Twayne's United States Authors Series

Sylvia E. Bowman, *Editor*

INDIANA UNIVERSITY

Ellen Glasgow

ELLEN GLASGOW

by **BLAIR ROUSE**
University of Arkansas

 26

Twayne Publishers, Inc.   ::   New York

IN MEMORY OF
ALICE WHITMER ROUSE
AND
HENRY EDWARD BUTTON
STAUNCH VIRGINIANS OF AN OLDER SCHOOL

Preface

IN THIS STUDY I present those facts, analyses, and interpretations which should make clear the manner of Ellen Glasgow's life, the nature and purposes of her writing, the scope of her work, and her attainments as an artist in fiction. I do not neglect the fact that she was Virginian and Southern as well as American, but I emphasize the wider implications of her life and her novels.

In the first chapter of *Ellen Glasgow*, "Shapes and Shapers," I present the significant biographical material pertinent to an understanding of the novelist as woman and artist: those elements of experience in childhood, youth, and maturity which made her the person she was and which guided and shaped her imagination. In the second chapter, "The Novelist and Her Art," I trace the development of the novelist's theory and practice of the art of prose fiction and present, to a considerable extent in her own words, her ideas and opinions about that art. In chapters three through nine, I discuss each of Ellen Glasgow's novels, providing summaries of the stories, analyses of the significant elements, and estimates of the importance of the books both individually and in relation to the novelist's whole achievement. Finally, in chapter ten, I offer a survey of the critical reception of Ellen Glasgow and her work and a brief summary of her significance for the art of the novel in America.

I cannot thank all who have in some way aided me. I should be sure to omit inadvertently the name of someone who had provided valuable assistance during the years in which I have been particularly interested in Ellen Glasgow. I wish, however, to express appreciation to a few persons to whom I am especially indebted for assistance which contributed more directly to the preparation of this volume: Miss Georgia Clark and Mrs. Katherine Hantz of the Reference Department of the Library of the University of Arkansas; Mr. John Cooke Wiley of the Alderman Library of the University of Virginia; Mrs. Julia S. Bigham, literary executor for Marjorie Kinnan Rawlings; Mrs. Irita Van Doren, literary executor for Ellen Glasgow; the Research Committee of the College of Arts and Sciences of the University of

Arkansas; two fellow Glaswegians, Professor William W. Kelly of Michigan State University and Professor Frederick P. W. McDowell of the State University of Iowa, for generously sharing their interest in and knowledge of Ellen Glasgow; Professor James Southall Wilson of the University of Virginia, for sharing with me his memories of Ellen Glasgow and his knowledge of her work as well as for permission to quote from his writing about her; my friends Murrie Bates and Edward F. Overton of Richmond, Virginia, for on-the-spot research assistance; and my family and colleagues, especially Professors Claude Faulkner, Leighton Rudolph, and Leo Van Scyoc, for enduring my presence while I wrote this book.

For permission to quote from the works of Ellen Glasgow, including *Letters of Ellen Glasgow,* which I edited, I am grateful to Harcourt, Brace & World, Inc. (formerly Harcourt, Brace & Co., Inc.), who control the rights to these books. I am grateful also to Mr. Luther Y. Gore for permission to consult his edition of an article by Ellen Glasgow, "Literary Realism or Nominalism," *American Literature,* XXXIV (March, 1962), 72-79; to Professor James B. Colvert, author, and to Professor Fredson Bowers, editor, for permission to use material from "Author and Agent: Ellen Glasgow's Letters to Paul Revere Reynolds," *Studies in Bibliography,* XIV (1961), 177-96; to Professor Thomas H. English for permission to use my article originally published in the *Emory University Quarterly,* VI (March, 1950), 30-40; and to Col. C. C. Tutwiler, Jr., for permission to consult his paper on Ellen Glasgow's reading; to Dr. L. Beverley Chaney, president of the Joseph Collins Foundation and executor of the estate of Dr. Joseph Collins, for permission to quote from Dr. Collins' work as indicated in the notes. I am grateful to the following publishers of periodicals and books for permission to quote from their publications as indicated in the notes: the publishers of *The Atlantic Monthy, College English, The New York Herald Tribune, The New York Times, Saturday Review* (formerly *The Saturday Review of Literature*), *Time, The Virginia Quarterly Review,* and Doubleday & Company.

BLAIR ROUSE

January 27, 1962
University of Arkansas
Fayetteville

Contents

Chronology

1873   Ellen Glasgow born, April 22, in Richmond, Virginia, at 101 East Cary St.

1880   Becomes a writer in her seventh summer, at "Jerdone's Castle."

1888   Moves from birthplace at 101 East Cary St. to One West Main St.

1889   Hearing begins to fade.

1890   Had written some four hundred pages of a novel, *Sharp Realities*, which she later destroyed.

1891   Begins writing *The Descendant*.

1893   Ellen Glasgow's mother dies October 27; Ellen destroys part of *The Descendant*.

1895   Returns to undestroyed portion of *The Descendant* and completes the novel.

1896   First trip to Europe: sees England, Scotland and France that summer.

1897   *The Descendant* anonymously published in January.

1898   *Phases of an Inferior Planet* published in March.

1899   On long trip to Europe and the Middle East, February 4 to September 5. Winter of 1899-1900 falls in love with man she called Gerald B—— in *The Woman Within*.

1900   *The Voice of the People* published in April.

1902   *The Battle-Ground* published in March; *The Freeman and Other Poems* published in August.

1903   In Europe with sisters Rebe and Cary.

1904   *The Deliverance* published in January; in Europe with Rebe.

1905   In Europe; Gerald B—— dies.

1906   *The Wheel of Life* published in January; in Quebec in September.

1907 Spends summer in Italy.

1908 *The Ancient Law* published in January; in Italy and England.

1909 *The Romance of a Plain Man* published in January; in England in spring. Frank, Ellen Glasgow's brother, dies April 7.

1910 In France and Italy with sister, Cary. Miss Anne Virginia Bennett comes to Glasgow home to nurse the ill Cary.

1911 *The Miller of Old Church* published in May. Cary dies August 19.

1913 *Virginia* published in April.

1914 In Europe until shortly before outbreak of war; traveled over England.

1915 First met Henry Watkins Anderson (the Harold S—— of *The Woman Within*).

1916 Her father, Francis Thomas Glasgow, dies January 29. *Life and Gabriella* published in January.

1917 Ellen Glasgow and Henry W. Anderson engaged.

1918 Ellen Glasgow and Henry W. Anderson quarrel on July 3; that night she takes an overdose of sleeping tablets.

1919 Engagement of Ellen Glasgow and Henry W. Anderson broken. *The Builders* published in October.

1920 Becomes member of Phi Beta Kappa at College of William and Mary on December 4.

1922 *One Man in His Time* published in May.

1923 *The Shadowy Third and Other Stories* published in October.

1924 Becomes president of the Richmond Society for the Prevention of Cruelty to Animals; had long been active in humane campaigning.

1925 *Barren Ground* published in April.

1926 *The Romantic Comedians* published in September.

1927 In England in summer. Visits Thomas Hardy, Hugh Walpole, and Frank Swinnerton.

1929   *They Stooped to Folly* published in November.

1930   Receives degree of Doctor of Letters from University of North Carolina, June 10. In England and France.

1932   Elected to National Institute of Arts and Letters. *The Sheltered Life* published in September.

1935   *Vein of Iron* published in August.

1937   Spends June in Italy; her last trip to Europe.

1938   Receives degree of Doctor of Laws from the University of Richmond, April 29, and the same degree from Duke University, June 6. Virginia Edition of her novels published in July. Elected to membership in American Academy of Arts and Letters in December.

1939   Receives degree of Doctor of Laws from College of William and Mary, June 5. Heart attack in December.

1940   Second severe heart attack in spring. Award of Howells Medal announced November 15 by American Academy of Arts and Letters.

1941   *In This Our Life* published in March. Receives the *Saturday Review of Literature* Award for Distinguished Service to American Literature, April 5.

1942   Awarded Pulitzer Prize for fiction for 1941 for *In This Our Life*, May 5.

1943   *A Certain Measure*, her book of prefaces, published in October.

1945   Died on November 21, aged seventy-two, at her home at One West Main Street, Richmond, Virginia.

1954   *The Woman Within*, her autobiography, published in November.

1958   *Letters of Ellen Glasgow*, edited by Blair Rouse, published in January.

Ellen Glasgow

CHAPTER 1

Shapes and Shapers

ELLEN GLASGOW, the daughter of Francis Thomas Glasgow, came from Scotch-Irish pioneers who settled in western Virginia in the eighteenth century.[1] These hardy men, staunch Calvinists, hewed a place for civilization out of the wilderness. In or out of the pulpit, they were devoted to metaphysical inquiry. Although Ellen Glasgow rejected the harshness which characterized her father's faith, she inherited much of his Scotch-Irish strength of personality and took pride in this heritage. In two novels, *Barren Ground* and *Vein of Iron,* she delineated the virtues as well as the weaknesses of her Scotch-Irish forebears.

Through her mother, Anne Jane Gholson, Ellen Glasgow came from Tidewater Virginia aristocratic stock. From her mother she believed that she had received tolerance, social awareness, and the sensitivity of aristocratic birth and traditions. She also thought that she was born of a union of antipathetic personalities and traditions and that in her struggled an eternal conflict of these heritages.

Ellen Glasgow's earliest environment was that of her large family. Born in 1873, she was next to the youngest in a family of four sons and six daughters. The young Ellen had little in common with her older brothers and sisters. Of her older sisters, only with Cary did she ever have a true sympathy, and this intimacy did not develop until after Ellen's early childhood. In her childhood she found companionship only with her younger sister, Rebe.

I *The Lonely Youth*

Although she thought of childhood as a lonely time, Ellen Glasgow also enjoyed then the companionship of Mammy Lizzie Jones, her Negro nurse. To her the child Ellen was indebted for warm affection and for an exciting introduction to the world beyond her home. Through her she knew the streets and parks, the other Negro servants, and the varied ordinary folk of her town.

Ellen Glasgow's childhood did, nevertheless, contain more than a measure of loneliness. Her ill health often prevented her from joining other children in their amusements. Although her health also interfered with her education, her dislike for schoolroom procedures probably limited her formal education. She attended private schools in her neighborhood; but once she had learned to read, most of her learning came from her father's library.

In early life Ellen Glasgow knew a Richmond which preserved some of the amenities of a small Southern town: the closely knit neighborhoods in which lived people of comparable social and economic status; the acceptance of the stratification which clearly defined the several classes; the available Negro servants who provided labor for an insignificant wage and instructed white children in the code of manners by which they would be expected to live. Yet Richmond was a city in which the code of polite behavior was no longer all-sufficient for the aristocrat and had little meaning for the rising lower class.

She knew the people of her own class intimately, sympathetically, more often bitterly; she knew the lower orders of Virginia citizens less intimately. Throughout her fiction the poorer white people of Virginia have important roles, and usually they are clearly and accurately revealed. They are, nevertheless, persons who have been observed; they are not the author's own people. But they have been observed from a much closer vantage point than were the New England folk whom Edith Wharton introduced into her fiction.

Ellen Glasgow looked back upon her youth and early maturity as a time of sadness and of spiritual as well as physical torment. The illness and death of her mother when Ellen Glasgow was twenty brought her the first of several deep sorrows. The deaths of her brother Frank, of George McCormack, Cary's husband, and then of Cary herself, all were overwhelming blows. After each death, however, she struggled free of the despair which threatened to sweep over her. After her mother's death, her situation was even more difficult because of the estrangement between Ellen Glasgow and her father and between her and her older sisters, with the exception of Cary. She rebelled against the religious observances of these older members of her family and refused to go to church. Nor would she surrender to them in their objections to her reading material, much of which her father and sisters regarded as heretical if not actually atheistic.

Ellen Glasgow's associations with family and friends were important in her own experience and for her fiction. She seems to have adored her mother and possibly hated her father. For her mother she felt mingled admiration, sentimental affection, and dependence for protection from a harsh world and for understanding of her difficulties and desires. Lost, overwhelmed, she was ill in the months following her mother's death and withdrew more and more into herself.

Her antipathy for her father may indeed have been hate. When she wrote of their relationship in *The Woman Within*, she tried to be fair to him; yet she did not minimize the discord which had existed. She resented her father's insensitivity to animals, and she never forgave his disposing of the dogs and of a horse which she and her mother had cherished. Even stronger was her antipathy toward his religion, or to the harsher features of his Presbyterianism as she saw them exhibited in her home.

Only with Cary did she find sympathy as well as intellectual similarity of tastes. Both Cary and her husband encouraged the young novelist in her reading. Their gift of a subscription to the Mercantile Library of New York enabled Ellen Glasgow to choose books other than those available to her in Richmond. Cary also encouraged her in her writing and aided in finding a publisher for her work. With her younger sister, Rebe, and with Cary, Ellen Glasgow enjoyed her happiest family relationships after her mother's death.

With her brothers, Frank and Arthur, Ellen Glasgow was never closely associated. Frank's tormented nature constituted a barrier to intimacy. In their mature years, Ellen and Arthur seem to have respected each other. He owned the home at One West Main Street, and his aid in maintaining the house, as well as in other ways, was apparently gratefully accepted.

In spite of her youthful sadness, Ellen Glasgow never became an embittered recluse. She enjoyed dances at Virginia Military Institute and the University of Virginia; she bowed to the society of Charleston at a St. Cecilia's Ball. She visited the Virginia springs, entertained in Richmond, and shared in the charitable activity expected of a young lady of good family. Not too carefully chaperoned, she visited New York for the opera as well as for visits to an aurist and a literary agent. And when she was twenty-three, she made the first of a number of trips abroad.

II A Hampering Affliction

Associated with Ellen Glasgow's youth, but sustained as a hated burden throughout life, was the deafness which appeared when she was sixteen. At first physicians insisted there was no danger of loss of hearing, but the deafness grew worse. For the rest of her life, she sought relief from pain and assistance in hearing. Much of her nervous difficulty was surely related to her struggle, for she never became reconciled to her condition. Only toward the end of her life did she find a hearing aid which she could use with some ease. Because of her disability, she was not able to travel alone. This situation hampered her independence, restricted her movements, and made traveling exceedingly expensive. Her deafness may have made her hesitant to marry. Certainly she became extremely sensitive about her condition and bitterly resented any mention of her deafness in print.

How much deafness and poor health affected Ellen Glasgow's writing must be a matter of speculation. Although she did use aural images to some extent, especially in her earlier novels, she employed visual imagery to a far greater extent. One probable result of her poor health may be the presence in her fiction of important characters who suffer physical or psychic wounds. It seems other than simple coincidence that illness or injury figures importantly in the lives of the central characters in *The Descendant* and *Phases of an Inferior Planet*—her first published novels— and in such other books as *The Ancient Law, Virginia, Life and Gabriella, The Builders, Barren Ground, The Romantic Comedians, The Sheltered Life, Vein of Iron,* and *In this Our Life.*

Some of Ellen Glasgow's more rewarding characters are persons, usually men, who have been harshly wounded physically or psychically. One of these is Uncle Tucker Corbin, the maimed Civil War veteran of *The Deliverance.* In an otherwise bitter novel, he breathes kindness, good sense, and an awareness of beauty. He is the first of Ellen Glasgow's "civilized" men, all of whom have suffered some deep injury yet have learned how to live fruitful lives: Marmaduke Littlepage, the maimed painter of *They Stooped to Folly;* General Archbald of *The Sheltered Life,* whose childhood spiritual wound molded his existence; John

Fincastle of *Vein of Iron,* whose "wound" may seem ambiguous but no less evident; and Asa Timberlake of *In This Our Life,* whose life was a long humiliation yet who knew values and how to live a mean life without acquiring the taint of meanness.

A set of "ill" women reflects Ellen Glasgow's preoccupation with her uncertain health and deafness and her recognition, possibly subconscious, of her own tendency to surrender to illness. Some of these women refuse to give in to illness: Marthy Burr in *The Voice of the People,* Ben Starr's mother in *The Romance of a Plain Man,* Mrs. Oakley in *Barren Ground,* and Mary Evelyn in *Vein of Iron.* Others, however, use frail health as an instrument of their tyranny over others, especially men: Angela in *The Miller of Old Church* and Angelica in *The Builders* (the irony of the names may be too obvious); Lavinia, of *In This Our Life,* the insufferable wife of Asa. One may see in the creation of these characters the novelist's own therapeutic act. Perhaps she imagined in these women the horrible person she herself might become if she surrendered completely to her frail health or used it as a weapon.

III *Love and Friendships*

Ellen Glasgow's most intimate friend was Mrs. Carrie Coleman Duke. After Mr. Glasgow purchased "Jerdone's Castle" from Carrie Coleman's father, the Colemans continued to live on an adjoining farm. The two small girls became close friends. Later Carrie Coleman Duke lived in Richmond within a short distance of One West Main Street. After the novelist returned to Richmond from her New York sojourn to settle permanently in her old home, she depended upon Mrs. Duke for companionship in her travels as well as for the strength of her warm personality. Mrs. Duke, an intelligent woman with a keen interest in people, had little interest in literature but was an expert dealer in antiques. The two Southern ladies seem to have complemented each other.

Differing in scope and nature from her friendship with Mrs. Duke was Ellen Glasgow's association with Anne Virginia Bennett. Miss Bennett, a trained nurse, came to the Glasgow home to nurse Cary in her last illness. She remained with Ellen as companion, housekeeper, secretary, and friend. On her capable shoulders rested the burden of running the house, providing the elaborate entertainment for which One West Main Street became known, and, most important, of guarding Ellen Glasgow from annoyance and the interruption of her work. Anne Virginia took care of the business details; she copied the novelist's rough drafts, and often retyped them many times before Ellen Glasgow was satisfied with a passage; she also looked after the succession of dogs which inhabited the old house. Ellen Glasgow delighted in, loved, and wept over pets; but Miss Bennett took care of them.

Other friends in Richmond brought pleasure and emotional sustenance to Ellen Glasgow. It is not clear, however, that any of her closest intimates among the women she knew in Richmond exercised any direct influence upon her art as a novelist. But several of her male acquaintances did have such an influence. In her mid-twenties Ellen Glasgow loved the man whom she called Gerald B—— in her autobiography. Her love for him was ecstatically passionate, but of the precise nature of their relationship and of the identity of her lover she remained ambiguous. She wrote of him as an older man with a wife and children, as a "Wall Street" man, as one whom she met in New York and Europe. Evidence other than her autobiography suggests that her lover was a physician rather than a businessman.[2] Her love revealed itself in the novelist's work. One sees richness, growing maturity, and self-confidence in the novels written during the period of her love with Gerald B——. *The Voice of the People, The Battle-Ground,* and *The Deliverance* suggest that she was discovering a new source of emotion and insight into human relationships. When her love for this man was thwarted by his death (whatever might otherwise have been its outcome), her grief and the ensuing disturbance of her emotions and imagination probably account for the fact that *The Wheel of Life* and *The Ancient Law* are inferior to those novels which had immediately preceded them. Of these, Ellen Glasgow later admitted that *The Wheel of Life* was directly autobiographical, was written much too close to time and events, and was, as a result, a poor work of fiction.

Ellen Glasgow later experienced several other serious attachments to men. One was with a man whom she knew, liked, and respected when she lived in New York, although he was of another social stratum; he became the model for O'Hara, the Irish businessman in *Life and Gabriella.* When she spent the summer in California in 1915, she experienced a passing infatuation for a man she met there. A third affair was with the man to whom she became engaged for a brief moment following her love with Gerald B——. In her memoirs she frankly stated that she entered into this engagement experimentally and quickly decided not to marry the man.

One other of Ellen Glasgow's loves affected her deeply: her affair with the man to whom she referred as Harold S—— and who was Henry Watkins Anderson, an eminent Richmond lawyer. Of this friendship and love she wrote at length in *The Woman Within* as a woman who had loved affectionately and with respect, and who had been deeply hurt. She met Mr. Anderson in 1915, became engaged to him in 1917, and broke the engagement in 1919. In the meantime Mr. Anderson had been in Roumania administering Red Cross assistance in distressed areas and enjoying the honors bestowed by royalty and others of high rank.

In her cutting narrative of her affair with "Harold S——," Ellen Glasgow implies that her engagement was broken and the friendship ended. This was not exactly the case, for the association continued for many years. Mr. Anderson was frequently a dinner guest at One West Main Street, and the two people continued to correspond; or certainly Mr. Anderson wrote to Ellen Glasgow, for among his letters to her is one dated some two weeks before her death. Yet the novelist could never forgive him for the hurt she had experienced. In *The Woman Within* Mr. Anderson is made to appear silly, pompous, and a completely self-centered place-seeker. Curiously mingled with these impressions are evidences that he was also a man of intelligence, energy, perspicacity, and integrity. That he was a self-made man Ellen Glasgow did not hold against him; yet she made this fact the basis for passages suggesting that he was a fatuous social-climber who assumed "airs" of grandeur to the amusement of the older families of Richmond. All this would surely have been most painful to Mr. Anderson had he ever seen these pages, but *The Woman Within* was not published until he and the novelist were dead. Ellen Glasgow seems not to have considered the feelings of Mr. Anderson's family of nieces and nephews.

Ellen Glasgow's experience with Henry Anderson had other direct bearing upon her work. *The Builders,* published in 1919 and written during her engagement, evinces ideas and feelings related to Mr. Anderson. David Blackburn in the novel was clearly modeled upon him in that Blackburn was a self-made man of ability who aspired to political leadership. Physically Anderson was not like Blackburn, nor did his life contribute details to the plot. In another respect he influenced *The Builders* in an unfortunate manner: in the passages devoted to Blackburn's letters or monologues, Ellen Glasgow presented material drawn directly from Anderson's conversations about political matters. He attests as much in his letters to her in which he seems to regret that she had so explicitly used his words and ideas, but he also indicates in other letters that he had read large portions of the novel while it was in progress and had approved of it enthusiastically.[3] In any case, *The Builders* is a poor novel made poorer because of its involvement in vague, muddled political emphasis.

After the breaking of the engagement, Henry Anderson ran for governor of Virginia on the Republican ticket, a gallant gesture which met its almost inevitable defeat at the hands of the Democratic machine. A speech by Ellen Glasgow favoring the Republican ticket survives in half-finished form among her papers at the University of Virginia. Hers is a vigorous, enthusiastic address, though she does not mention Henry Anderson by name. It is not evident that she ever delivered the address.[4]

One Man in His Time, published in 1922, is also involved in Ellen Glasgow's affair with Henry Anderson: it depicts not only a self-made governor of Virginia, who has risen from obscure origins, but an eminent lawyer, the political opponent of Governor Vetch. This lawyer fails in love and politics because of spiritual flaws in his character. In a curious fashion, Ellen Glasgow used her lawyer-lover-friend as the model for both characters.

By 1922, when she began work on *Barren Ground*, Ellen Glasgow had partly recovered from her "tragic" experience with Anderson which for a time not only interrupted her career but came very close to ruining it. After her recovery she believed that her emotions and her mind had been deepened, enriched, and strengthened by all that she had endured. She determined to draw upon her emotional experience for character and action, and much of the woman that Ellen Glasgow had become went into the portrayal of Dorinda Oakley in *Barren Ground*. Much of the harshness and bitterness as well as the strength of that book derive from her view of herself and of her existence after the loss of love.

In still another book Ellen Glasgow reacted to her affair with

Henry Anderson: *The Romantic Comedians* sounds her scornful laughter at the pretensions of the elderly man who yearns for a young bride. Judge Honeywell is not Henry Anderson. But Ellen Glasgow's ironic scorn for the foolish aspirations of the male is born of the bitterness of her associations with the man whom she called Harold S——.

The extent and nature of Ellen Glasgow's other associations are suggested by what she says of them in her memoirs and her letters. In the last quarter-century of her life, she was closely associated with James Branch Cabell and Douglas Southall Freeman in Richmond and with James Southall Wilson in Charlottesville, Virginia. Cabell she had known slightly when they were both very young, but their close friendship developed in their more mature years. Each admired and respected the other; each commented on the other's work. Apparently she valued Cabell's advice and criticism of her work even though she did not follow his advice. Toward the end of her life came an estrangement which was only partly healed, and possibly this led her to introduce into *The Woman Within* unnecessary and bitter passages concerning him. Mr. Cabell, who survived Ellen Glasgow by several years, had the last ugly word in his rather ambiguous essay about his long-time friend in *As I Remember It*.

In Douglas Southall Freeman, Ellen Glasgow found an admiring friend and critic. She recognized his achievement as a historian and valued his good word in the articles he wrote about her. A somewhat comparable relationship existed between Ellen Glasgow and James Southall Wilson, professor of English at the University of Virginia and founder-editor of *The Virginia Quarterly Review*. She valued his essays about her books, for she recognized in him a critic who enjoyed and admired her novels but who would speak of them truthfully and forthrightly. Such criticism she did not always accept gracefully; for she did not find it easy in her later years, when she often fancied herself neglected, to accept anything less than complete and unqualified admiration from those critics she considered her friends.

To the friendships of Ellen Glasgow's later years and their importance to her, the pages of her letters and her memoirs testify eloquently. Some of these were people in New York literary circles whom she valued as persons but from whom she also sought support in gaining the recognition she believed her books deserved. Of such a semi-professional nature were her associations with J. Donald Adams, of *The New York Times;* Irita Van Doren, of *The New York Herald Tribune;* Henry Seidel Canby, of *The Saturday Review of Literature;* Howard Mumford Jones; Stark Young; Allen Tate; Carl Van Vechten; H. L. Mencken and his wife, Sara Haardt; Van Wyck Brooks; and Charles Hanson Towne. With all these she enjoyed rewarding friendships as well as, in varying degree, the critical support she sought for her work.

In Mrs. Van Doren, in Marion Gausse Canby, wife of H. S. Canby, and in Bessie Zaban Jones, wife of H. M. Jones, she found the more intimate understanding of intelligent women to whom she could talk and write of matters close to her. In Signe Toksvig, the Danish wife of the critic Francis Hackett and an author in her own right, Ellen Glasgow found a friend to whom she could write of spiritual, intellectual, and literary concerns. Her friendships with Mrs. Van Doren and Van Wyck Brooks were warmer and more personally rooted than with some of her other literary friends.

Of the American women novelists of her time, Ellen Glasgow knew well only Mary Johnston, the friend of her earlier days, and Marjorie Kinnan Rawlings, with whom she became closely associated toward the end of her life. She especially liked *The Yearling* and found in Mrs. Rawlings a sympathetic understanding. In turn, Mrs. Rawlings admired Ellen Glasgow and planned to write her biography, a work cut off by Mrs. Rawlings' death.

Apparently, Ellen Glasgow never cared to meet Edith Wharton and Willa Cather. Though she was circumspect in her references to these contemporaries, she seemingly had no affection for either of them, least of all for Willa Cather. Possibly surprising is the fact that she was not favorably impressed by the work of Elizabeth Madox Roberts, whose *The Time of Man* has much in common with *Barren Ground*. She said Miss Roberts' "writing seems to me overstrained and unrelated to the life she portrays."[5]

Over the years Ellen Glasgow knew and sometimes admired several foreign writers. She was strongly drawn both to Thomas Hardy and Joseph Conrad; she liked Frank Swinnerton and his wife. Of these writers only Hardy exercised an influence upon her fiction, and this influence had made itself felt in her earlier work sometime before she met the aging novelist. Though she never met Virginia Woolf, she greatly admired her work. John Galsworthy and Arnold Bennett she knew and liked. Radclyffe Hall, author of *The Well of Loneliness,* she respected and admired. With Hugh Walpole, who in the 1920's enjoyed an extraordinary popularity in America, Ellen Glasgow experienced a lively friendship and carried on an interesting correspondence. Walpole visited her several times in Richmond, where he was lionized to his great content. Their friendship ended abruptly when he reneged on his invitation to her to visit him in England.[6]

IV   *Travels*

Ellen Glasgow traveled extensively. After her first trip to Britain in 1896, she crossed the Atlantic a number of times on journeys which took her to most of Europe, outside of Russia, and to the Mediterranean regions. Switzerland was associated with her love affair with Gerald B——. England and Italy she loved more than any of the other countries of Europe, and she delighted in returning to England as often as opportunity permitted. From time to time she enjoyed vacations in Quebec and Prince Edward Island.

Her own country Ellen Glasgow knew only in part. Virginia, of course, she knew intimately. Other regions of the South she knew slightly. She visited North Carolina but never Florida, although her friend Marjorie Kinnan Rawlings urged her to do so. Her vacations usually took her to the Virginia springs, to Atlantic City, or to spots in Connecticut, in Massachusetts (Nantucket), or in Maine. California she visited in the summer of 1915, and she looked back upon her stay in San Francisco with keen pleasure. In the latter twenties and early thirties she entertained a lively antipathy toward the Midwest; but this was more a dislike of some of the fiction about that region than dislike for the region itself, about which she knew almost nothing. This she admitted when she was introduced to the poetry of Carl Sandburg and found in it much to admire.[7]

Ellen Glasgow's travel brought her pleasure and relief from troubles, but she did not draw upon her impressions of foreign lands and peoples for setting or characters. Only Virginia and its people adequately stimulated her imagination. Her fictional excursions beyond its borders were almost wholly unrewarding for reader and author.

V *Reading*

Ellen Glasgow read widely throughout her life.[8] When she was a child, the fairy stories of Hans Christian Andersen and of the Grimm brothers introduced her to the world of wonder. Scott's *Old Mortality* she liked to remember as her "first reader", later came all of his Waverley series. In her childhood she had also read Dickens; somewhat later she read the novels of Richardson and Fielding as well as the work of Defoe, Sterne, and Smollett. She believed that by the time she entered upon the profession of novelist she "had read every celebrated novel written in English."[9] She implies that as late as 1900 she had read little of Tolstoy and none of Turgenev, Chekhov, and Dostoevsky; those authors would come still later. She had read, however, Balzac, Flaubert, and Maupassant.[10] From Balzac and Flaubert she received her impetus toward the depiction of Virginia society in fiction, especially the areas of that life hitherto neglected: the lives of the lower middle class, the rural working classes, and the Negroes. In the work of these writers she also found the suggestion that she give a truthful account of Southern life rather than a gilded portrayal. Yet she may have derived her idea of what a novel really was far more from the nineteenth-century English novelists than from the French. Upon her British models she shaped most of her fiction before *Barren Ground,* but even this novel and others which follow it are not free from the influence of the Victorian novels she had read. Though she liked to think of herself as primarily a realist, Ellen Glasgow's work exhibits her romantic inclinations. It can be no surprise that she delighted in *Les Miserables* and the stories of Robert Louis Stevenson.

Other fiction which she mentions includes the work of Dumas, the Brontës, Jane Austen, Proust, Virginia Woolf, Henry James, and William Dean Howells. She early resolved that she did not wish to write a Howells novel nor a Henry James story. She enjoyed the work of Dumas, the Brontës, and Austen. Proust seems to have come too late to make a deep impression. She delighted in the work of Virginia Woolf and apparently found in Mrs. Woolf's technique suggestions for certain effects she developed in *The Sheltered Life* and *Vein of Iron,* notably in "The Deep Past" section of the former and in the several early chapters of the latter in which she evokes the inner lives of her characters.

As a young girl she encountered the work of John Stuart Mill,

Adam Smith, Sir Henry Maine, Malthus, Walter Bagehot, Henry George, and the histories of Lecky and Buckle. Later she read Karl Marx. Although she prided herself as a student of political economy, she recognized the greater influence in her thought of Darwin's *The Origin of Species* and of other nineteenth-century evolutionary writing. A central element in her belief was an inclination toward evolutionary principles, but her reaction to her reading of Darwin was more emotional than philosophical. She *felt* rather than believed in any clearly logical way.

She attained a belief in the possibility of *Goodness* and in the possible existence of a God of Love. In her youth she moved in her reading from materialistic, rationalistic exposition to the mysticism of the Orient and then to idealistic philosophy. Her interest in philosophic exploration led her to Schopenhauer, Kant, Fichte, Schelling, and later to Nietzsche and Herbert Spencer. She had delighted in Marcus Aurelius while rejecting Spinoza's too intellectualized world of the spirit. She read Oriental poetry and religious works with pleasure but showed little inclination toward mysticism except for an occasional interest in manifestations of the supernatural.

Although Ellen Glasgow read widely in political economy, the direct influence of this reading upon the complexion of her novels is not evident. In *The Voice of the People* and *The Miller of Old Church* she does little more than depict the emerging activity of the man of the lower classes in Virginia politics. In *One Man in His Time* she attempts a more complex involvement: the idealistic but relatively shallow political leader caught between his ideals on the one hand and the practical politicians of his own party and of the opposition on the other. In *The Builders* she echoes the ideas of Henry W. Anderson and devotes far too much of the novel to political essays in the form of monologues and letters. Yet what she says in the novel and in the speech already mentioned hardly constitutes a political philosophy: her love of Virginia; the need for doing what will be best for the Commonwealth; the necessity of electing the Republican ticket in order to overthrow the Democratic party now too long in power, lethargic and ineffectual; the desirability of electing the best men; and the need of two-party government to prevent the decadence almost inevitable when one party is too long in power.[11] Possibly in Nick Burr's admiration for Jefferson in *The Voice of the People* one finds an echo of Ellen Glasgow's admiration for Jeffersonian principles. Yet it remains that, although she wrote of political matters in several of her novels, Ellen Glasgow was not explicit concerning her own political theories or the political history of the situations in which her characters were portrayed.

From her early reading in political science and economics Ellen Glasgow developed what she considered very liberal, even "radical" views. Although she enjoyed thinking of herself as a radical, her "radicalism" was of a very mild variety. She exhibited no clear allegiance to socialism or other left-wing political and social developments of the turn of the century. Her political characters do not clearly exemplify any political theory held by the author other than her interest in the rise of the common man to political eminence. Ellen Glasgow's radicalism was little more than a spirit of rebellion against custom, sentimentality, and especially cruelty. As she grew older, she became somewhat more conservative. Occasionally, she uses the word "communist" as an epithet, but it has little political connotation and is more often a label for someone, often a critic, of whom she disapproved.

She participated in the woman suffrage movement in the early years of the century, helped found a woman suffrage society, wrote a few poems with a feminist emphasis, and took part in a woman suffrage parade in England in 1914. Her interest in feminism and the woman suffrage movement is evident in the character of Miss Matoaca Bland in *The Romance of a Plain Man*. It is a mistake, however, to consider Ellen Glasgow as a thoroughgoing feminist. She wanted women to have the right to vote. Once that had been achieved, she had little interest in feminism. Only her humane society activity claimed her lifelong interest outside her work as novelist.

CHAPTER 2

The Novelist and Her Art

ELLEN GLASGOW thought seriously of why and how she worked, what she wished to accomplish, and to what extent she had achieved her goals. In her autobiographical books, *The Woman Within* and *A Certain Measure*, in her letters, and elsewhere, she had much to say about the art of fiction and her own endeavors in that art. Her ideas and opinions may provide a further revelation of the novelist as artist.

Ellen Glasgow devoted to her work the solicitude of the conscientious craftsman. She wrote in *The Woman Within* that at the age of seven "the one permanent interest, the single core of unity at the centre of my nature, was beginning to shape itself, and to harden. I was born a novelist, though I formed myself into an artist."[1] Near the end of her life, when she feared that she would not be able to complete *In This Our Life*, she wrote to Professor James Southall Wilson: "Since my only conscience is the literary conscience I could not bear to leave a good piece of work with the end unfinished."[2]

Some years earlier she had written to J. Donald Adams: "I suppose I am a born novelist, for the things I imagine are more vital and vivid to me than the things I remember."[3] When she wrote these words, she felt sorry for herself as a dedicated artist in a materialistic time and place, for in this letter she also said: "No one in the modern world is more lonely than the writer with a literary conscience."[4] Yet her consuming interest in her work was too strong to keep her from writing, no matter how great the disappointments. She told Stark Young: "After more than thirty years, I feel lost when I try to absorb myself, even for a few weeks, in other interests. I do find a satisfaction that keeps me alive, and I have never expected any returns or rewards that were not restricted to the work itself."[5] And little more than two

ELLEN GLASGOW

weeks before her death she was considering the possibility of undertaking another novel."[6]

Ellen Glasgow had not been so neglected as she sometimes liked to believe, nor was she unaware of the value of her work in the literary market place. She made a good bargain with her publishers, was very much the prima donna in insisting upon her "place" at the top of promotion plans, and amazingly active in enlisting the services of persons conveniently situated for providing favorable receptions for her books. But she would insist: "I had not in the beginning, and I have not now, the slightest interest in fiction as a trade. Only as a form of art has fiction ever concerned me."[7] She was a conscious artist, but she was also a professional writer with an acute understanding of sales and royalties.

I Fiction—An Illuminating Mirror

What, then, to Ellen Glasgow was the art to which she devoted a life? Essentially, it was a means through which she discovered and expressed the shape and meaning of reality. Through her art, she might, if she were alert and sensitive, reveal some of the deeper truths realized only through the imagination and understood only by those readers possessing the imaginative spirit. She believed that the chief end of the novel is "to increase our understanding of life and heighten our consciousness. To do this, writing must not only render experience, it must interpret and intensify the daily processes of living."[8] For her, she wrote, "the true and only purpose of fiction is the communication of ideas, of feeling, of vital experience. Beyond this a novel is entitled to be anything and everything, from a treatise on philosophy to an affair of the heart."[9] Ellen Glasgow did not wish, therefore, to be considered primarily a *Southern* novelist, and certainly not a local writer. Writing to Allen Tate, she said: "As you perceive, I was not concerned with the code of Virginia, but with the conventions of the world we call civilized."[10] She liked the statement of Howard Mumford Jones that: "She has not written of Virginia life, but of human life in Virginia."[11]

She believed that the writer of fiction must endow reality with that vital expression which communicates its meaning to others. She thought of the novel as a living entity, never as a mechanically arranged device. And she approached her definition of the

32]

necessities of the artist-novelist when she wrote: "The power to create life is the staple of fiction. When the novelist possesses this one thing needful, all else, or very nearly all else, may be acquired."[12] To her recognition of reality, life, and an unforced development of the work of art as imperative necessities, Ellen Glasgow added light, that ultimate requirement, when she wrote: "The true realists, I felt, must illuminate experience, not merely transcribe it; and so, for my own purpose, I defined the art of fiction as experience illuminated."[13]

What more did Ellen Glasgow seek in the novel? How did she measure greatness in fiction? First, she recognized that the great novel possessed a timeless quality which made it the possession of any age. "The great novels," she wrote, ". . . have never, in any place or period, belonged to a limited trend, or been circumscribed in scope by a fashion. For the great novels have marched with the years. They are the contemporaries of time."[14] Great fiction, for her, would possess "power, passion, pity, ecstasy and anguish, hope and despair . . . and the way to greatness leads beyond manner, beyond method, beyond movement, to some ultimate dominion of spirit. Even style, the essence of all great literature, is not a manufactured film but a vital fluid."[15]

Ellen Glasgow was aware of the novel as a form of poetry; it was related to all poetry and shaped from the lives of all mankind out of the elements which distinguish men and women as humanity. She knew also that, although the novel must have a timeless quality, it must be founded solidly in a particular place and time. She recognized the novel as that form of history which expresses man's awareness of himself when she wrote that ". . . the art of fiction has remained the most accurate mirror of the different stages in the pilgrimage of humanity . . . though the chief end of the novel is to create life, there is a secondary obligation which demands that fiction shall, in a measure at least, reflect the movement and the tone of its age."[16]

Clearly Ellen Glasgow meant to be a realist—at least in the sense that she understood realism. "I should have called myself a verist," she wrote later, "had such a term come my way."[17] She believed "that the whole truth must embrace the interior world as well as external appearances. Behaviour alone is only the outer envelope of personality; and this is why documentary realism, the notebook style, has produced merely surface impressions."[18] And she told me that she did not write from notes or from direct observation, although she took notes of words and phrases she wished to remember.[19] As she looked back upon the beginnings of her career, she thought that in writing of Virginia she had interpreted an intimately known realm and that she had been born knowing good and evil as well as hating inhumanity.[20]

How did her concept of the nature of her existence and of the time and place in which she lived shape the purpose of her art? In *The Woman Within* she said: ". . . I would write, I resolved, as no Southerner had ever written, of the universal chords beneath the superficial variations of scene and character. I would write of all the harsher realities beneath manners, beneath social customs, beneath the poetry of the past, and the romantic nostalgia of the present. . . . I would take as my theme those ugly aspects of life the sentimentalists passed over."[21]

From the beginning of her career Ellen Glasgow determined to avoid sentimentality and the kind of idealism which she called evasive. At first this determination led her away from the South for her materials. When she wrote her two apprentice novels, *The Descendant* and *Phases of an Inferior Planet,* she laid the scene in New York; but she was never at ease with this setting. She came to believe that for every writer there was a country of the mind and that hers was "the familiar Virginian scene of my childhood."[22] And so Ellen Glasgow wrote of those scenes familiar to her, especially those she had known as a child: Richmond; the borderland of the Piedmont and Tidewater regions around the Glasgow farm, "Jerdone's Castle"; the Valley of Virginia; and the Tidewater country. For some of her books she studied thoroughly the setting as she found it in her own time and as she could imagine it in the time of her story. For several of her later novels she created Queenborough, which embodied the essence of Virginia towns as she understood them. Anyone familiar with Richmond, however, will recognize that city in Ellen Glasgow's Queenborough.

Her concern with setting is plain in her comments concerning the old town which she called Dinwiddie in *Virginia* but which Virginians know as Petersburg: "My Dinwiddie was saturated with the breath of old streets and old houses. . . . The place in my mind had wholeness, solidity, the capacity for extension."[23] She emphasized in her conversations with me, the importance of her childhood memories—especially those of the summers she had spent at "Jerdone's Castle" in Louisa County. She spoke of the broomsedge that grew there and of its varied beauty in the changing seasons. Her delight in this grass is interesting when we notice her sinister symbolic use of it in *Barren Ground.*

Although Ellen Glasgow turned consciously to write about Virginia surroundings and history in *The Voice of the People,* she had not envisioned that this book would become the first book of her social history of the Commonwealth in the form of fiction; but she had—she told me—consciously planned to write such a group of novels. As she had worked on *The Battle-Ground* and *The Deliverance,* she had become aware of the possibilities and had begun to develop the idea for the books which would trace the social history of Virginia. She thought that *The Voice of the People* was the first actually realistic novel to come from the South at the time she wrote it. At least, she insisted, she knew of no other then, and had not since learned of any in existence at that time.[24]

II *Reality and Art*

She realized that if she would write of the South in a way very different from those who had preceded her, her work would require another approach: "I would treat of the continual dissolution and renewal of social patterns, not in the South alone, but wherever man has built his temporary habitation in a universe that is indifferent or hostile."[25] She resented any implication that she was a romancer, though she recognized the necessity for writing truthfully of matters essentially romantic. She wrote to Joseph Hergesheimer: "My *Virginia* is as realistic as any production of the Middle West—only realism of that period in Virginia was tinctured with romantic illusion. But, I have always looked through a veil of irony even in the days when all fiction wore fancy dress."[26]

Some years later she wrote of her beginnings and her intentions: ". . . the South needed blood and irony. Blood it needed because Southern culture had strained too far away from its roots in the earth; it had grown thin and pale; it was satisfied to exist on borrowed ideas, to copy instead of create. And irony is an indispensable ingredient of the critical vision; it is the safest antidote to sentimental decay."[27] Later she was convinced that she had begun writing too early, that she had needed more time for experience and perspective to mature: "It is not sufficient to test life; one should consume and assimilate it before one attempts to cast fresh experience into a permanent form."[28]

So Ellen Glasgow worked toward a method "which must be," she believed, "a method that was wholly unconscious, that had been, as it were, organized into an instinct. Although . . . I was ignorant of literary theories, I was, nevertheless, ripe for the invigorating influence of the first great realistic novelists, whose books were then only beginning to be widely read in America."[29] The great realists of whom she spoke were Balzac, Flaubert, and Maupassant. From them she learned, among other things: ". . . that the assembling of material, the arrangement of masses, may have greater effect than the material itself. A wrong slant of light, a false point of view, a person or object out of focus, a slight failure in perspective—a single one of these errors may drain the life and colour from any landscape, from any figure . . . . the right arrangement of parts may bring out latent and unsuspected possibilities in the simplest scene or situation."[30]

Ellen Glasgow considered the true realists as "explorers of the heart"; from them she learned of the wide gulf existing between "the novel bearing a sincere emotion toward life" and "the novel that depends upon a sterile convention."[31] Possibly she would have developed her art more rapidly and more effectively had she come to the great Russian writers of the nineteenth century somewhat earlier, or had she been able to find more clearly in the English writers what she could adapt to her own needs. What the French realists could teach her was useful when she came upon it; its ultimate effect upon her work may have been unfortunate.

What more did the life of the artist in fiction mean to Ellen Glasgow? She thought of "that pre-established harmony between material and medium" as "the one unqualified reward in the pursuit of a difficult craft."[32] She also believed "the natural writer must, of necessity, live on the surface the life of accepted facts, which is the life of action and shadows, while with his deeper consciousness he continues to live that strangely valid life of the mind, which is related to the essence of things in themselves and to the more vivid world of the imagination."[33] Her ultimate aim she expressed once in these words: "Humanity and distinction, reality and art—these are the special qualities for which I have striven throughout my work."[34]

Ellen Glasgow believed that good novels could be written in America "by those novelists who are concerned more with the quality of excellence than with the characteristic of Americanism."[35] America, she thought, was large enough to take in "the diverse qualities in all novels ever written by American novelists at home or abroad."[36] She would not accept the notion that there was anything especially significant in her material because it was Southern. She wrote:

> . . . Wherever humanity has taken root there has been created, . . . the stuff of great novels; and this is true of the South in the exact degree that it is true of every other buried past upon earth. But it is even truer that wherever the predestined artist is born his material is found awaiting his eyes and his hand. All that is required, indeed, for the novel would appear to be a scene that is large enough to hold three characters, two passions, and one point of view.[37]

When she wrote of war, Ellen Glasgow chose not to write of adventure or romance, though these would be part of her materials, but "to make, as it were, a picture of varied characters who lived and loved and suffered . . . and to show the effects of the times upon the developments of their natures." She would show war as "merely an effective setting for a story of life."[38] She had determined ". . . to portray not Southern 'types' alone, but whole human beings, and to touch, or at least to feel for, the universal chords beneath regional variations of character. . . . I had learned that there are many facets of human nature and that the aspect we call the regional is only the universal surveyed from a shifted angle of vision."[39]

When she began to write seriously of the life that she understood, Ellen Glasgow recognized that the life of the lower classes of Southern white people offered a rich field for her art.[40] She told me that she had come to know these people well when she had lived in rural Virginia, so that she could capture the rhythms of their speech and appreciate their virtues as well as understand their weaknesses. She emphasized, as she makes clear in her novels, that she did not, usually, write of the lowest class of country people. Her poorer white people were not sharecroppers but small farmers who owned their own land and, with their families, farmed the places themselves. Though often illiterate, they were also frequently admirable people. She had known and admired the counterpart of Nick Burr in *The Voice of the People*."[41]

When she wrote *Barren Ground*, she treated a class of people almost entirely neglected in Southern fiction. These people were, for the most part, not "poor whites" in the usual sense of that term. They were land poor "good people," as distinguished from the members of "good families."[42] Nor did she consider agricultural matters so important in her novels as did imperceptive readers. "Systems of agriculture," she wrote, "were unimportant beside this human drama of love and hatred, of passion and disillusionment."[43]

Ellen Glasgow believed that traditional materials must offer something more to the artist than an opportunity to bestow memorials. "I still believe," she said, "that a heroic legend is the noblest creation of man. But I believe also that legend to be a blessing must be recreated not in funeral wreaths, but in dynamic tradition, and in the living character of a race. . . ."[44]

III *Character and Angle of Vision*

Concerning her choice of subject, theme, and character, Ellen Glasgow said that whenever she had ". . . tried to invent, rather than subconsciously create, a theme or a character, invariably the effort . . . resulted in failure. . . . Invariably the characters appear first, and slowly and gradually build up their own world, and spin the situation and atmosphere out of themselves. Strangely enough, the horizon of this real or visionary world is limited by the impressions or recollections of my early childhood."[45] She defended her use of Stanley and Roy as names for Asa's daughters in *In This Our Life*, pointing out that the use of family names for girls was a familiar practice in Virginia and insisting that once when she had tried to change Roy's name to Rhoda "she immediately went into a trance." She thought that "characters select their own names, or are born with them, and absolutely refuse to progress except on their own terms."[46]

The novelist's imperative task, Ellen Glasgow believed, is the creation of character. She expressed this concept in a letter to Hugh Walpole, saying:

> . . . Like you my one interest, apart from the quality of the thing as literature, is the creation of character—and of course, in the

most modern of the modernists, there are no cohesive characters, only a stream of more or less vague impressions or sensations. . . . By the way I've just read *Babbitt,* and I agree with you that it is better than *Main Street.* There is a character in it. Babbitt, common as he is, because of his commonness perhaps, lives.[47]

When I talked with Ellen Glasgow, she did not deny that many of her women characters are stronger than her men. But she did deny that she had consciously designed them as stronger figures. Rather she thought that the growth of her women into stronger characters was implicit in the nature of the persons and the situations as well as in the subjects of the novels. We talked of *The Sheltered Life,* and I mentioned that Jenny Blair (a vivid characterization, though a weak person among Ellen Glasgow's women) developed as the reader followed her through the novel. Ellen Glasgow agreed and seemed pleased that I had noticed this. Then she went on to emphasize the necessity of growth and change for giving life to characters in a novel and the necessity that fictional characters live.[48]

One of Ellen Glasgow's favorite character patterns was that of the civilized person. "This rare pattern of mankind," she said, "has always attracted me as a novelist. I like to imagine how the world would appear if human beings were really civilized, not by machinery alone, but through that nobler organ which has been called the heart in the intellect."[49] Of Asa in *In This Our Life* she wrote, "I was depicting, not a failure in life, but a man in whom character, not success, was an end in itself."[50]

With her interest in evolutionary philosophy, Ellen Glasgow was naturally concerned with the relation of heredity and environment to character. Her "own theory . . . inclined to the belief that environment more than inheritance determines character. What it does not determine is the tendency of native impulse nurtured by tradition and legend, unless tradition and legend may be considered a part of environment."[51] She expressed comparable ideas to me and illustrated her position by suggesting that in *The Deliverance* she had shown character overcoming environment in the persons of the Blakes. She emphasized that she believed environment more powerful than heredity and thought she had illustrated this also in that novel.[52]

Closely related to her use of characters are Ellen Glasgow's ideas concerning form, structure, and point of view in fiction. As a general principle, she insisted "the book must have a form. This is essential. . . ."[53] "In *The Sheltered Life*, where I knew intuitively that the angle of vision must create the form, I employed two points of view alone, though they were separated by the whole range of experience."[54] She believed that in *Barren Ground* Dorinda Oakley had controlled both form and point of view, as in *The Sheltered Life* the child, Jenny Blair, and her grandfather, General Archbald, had shaped the structure of that novel. In her earlier books, the reader must usually, however, follow a shifting view of the action as seen through the minds of several characters, for only in *The Deliverance* and in *The Romance of a Plain Man*, among these earlier works, did she consider seriously the effect of point of view. This practice may not seem to agree with her saying that "Instinct alone had warned me that a narrative should adhere to the central figure, and that looseness of structure, as well as thinning substance, was the result of too variable a field of vision."[55] Instinct was insufficient for the young novelist; some of her earlier novels suffer from looseness of structure and a certain diffuseness. In *The Deliverance* she employed the country lawyer, Carraway, to provide a point of view not that of the author nor of an important character. Of this, her only use of the indirect approach, she said: "In a measure, this perplexed yet sympathetic understanding shields Christopher, not only from the reader but also from the narrator, who stands invisible at a little distance."[56]

IV *Style and Technique*

Ellen Glasgow's preoccupation with problems of style and creative technique runs through all her comment about her art. She wrote in *A Certain Measure*: ". . . I felt that the style I needed must have something more than mere facility. It must be elastic and adaptable and equal, on occasion, to the more or less serious emergencies of fiction. . . . It should be recognized as a natural part of the organism, not as extraneous decoration which may be forcibly peeled off without impairing the whole structure."[57]

Shaping her style was for Ellen Glasgow a gradual, rather painful process. She recalled that after she had written her first novel she knew that she "wanted a steady control over . . . ideas and . . . material . . . a technique of working."[58] She sought suggestions for her method in the writings of Balzac, Flaubert, and Maupassant. In Balzac she perceived a sentimental quality that she thought rarely, if ever, observed by most of his critics, a quality that she did not like.[59] Flaubert she rejected because ". . . The hand of the master was too evident; his fingerprints were too visible on every paragraph. . . . Life . . . is not modeled in clay; it is not even dough, to be twisted and pinched into an artificial perfection. The twisting may be there in the novel, but it must not be visible; it must remain always below the surface of art."[60]

From Flaubert, Ellen Glasgow went on to read Maupassant. She wished that she might ". . . write a novel as perfect in every sentence as *Une Vie*. . . .Yet, even here, after the first wild enthusiasm had worn off, I felt that something was missing. . . . Surely the novel should be a form of art—but art was not enough. It must contain not only the perfection of art, but the imperfection of nature."[61] Further reading made her aware that "truth to art became in the end simple fidelity to one's own inner vision."[62] If she had learned from Maupassant "the value of the precious word, of the swift phrase, of cool and scrupulous observation," she "had found that the French sentences had a way of going to one's head too quickly, and . . . had turned from Flaubert and Maupassant to the sobering English tradition."[63]

For Ellen Glasgow, problems of style were inevitably and inextricably involved in the evocation of tone, atmosphere, space, and time. She thought that readers had not perceived that, in *Barren Ground,*

> . . . the elements of Time and Space are the dominant powers. From the beginning I tried to evoke a background of unlimited space, . . .
>
> The sense of time is more difficult to achieve, and since it cannot be forced, it remains, I think, the most important problem that confronts the writer of fiction. . . . this movement of time cannot be arranged; it must flow inevitably from the theme of the story, which continues to obey the laws of an imaginary universe. . . .[64]

I recall Ellen Glasgow's speaking of time and space in *Barren Ground* as being coexistent in their action. She said that she felt that in this novel time existed more as duration and sweep (which would be in keeping with the long vista-like aspects of the structure of the book). In *Vein of Iron,* however, she thought time possessed a more flowing, ever-moving aspect. She suggested that this varying treatment of time and space in these novels might have resulted because in *Vein of Iron* she had written of the mountains and the Valley of Virginia and then changed her scene to eastern Virginia, while in *Barren Ground* she had written of a wider, more level, sweeping country, a land where one might look off across wide, long, level or slightly rolling fields and woodlands.[65]

Ellen Glasgow was intensely interested in the problems of style and technique that she encountered in writing her comedies of manners. Discussing these matters as they related to *The Romantic Comedians,* she wrote: ". . . I felt instinctively, . . . that the form demanded a brief time-sequence, a limited scope, and a touch that was light, penetrating, satirical. . . . What I needed, . . . was a style that was neither soft and spongy nor so hard and brittle that it would flake off into epigrams."[66]

She wrote further of these problems with respect to *They Stooped to Folly.* The relations of meaning, tone, and style concerned her in this statement: ". . . sophisticated comedy should move fluently against a background which [is] civilized. Harmony [is] essential in the relation of the parts to the whole. A single figure, a single object that was out of value would destroy the tone and the visible rhythm. . . ."[67]

She recognized comparable problems which she had faced in shaping the material of her imagining into the novel she called *The Sheltered Life:* ". . . My task was the simple one of extracting from the situation every thread of significance, every quiver of vitality, every glimmer of understanding. . . . I could see, too, the fragile surface of a style that I must strive, however unsuccessfully, to make delicate yet unbreakable."[68]

For a different kind of novel, such as *Vein of Iron,* Ellen Glasgow recognized the need for a different style. She wrote to Stark Young:

> . . . I have tried to fit every sentence into the whole pattern, and I have used different rhythms for retrospection and for narrative or dialogue. For example, you noticed of course that in those five different reflections (or streams of consciousness), when my five characters were seated before the fire in the

manse, I used varying cadences, from the long slow rhythm of age . . . to the aimless staccato thinking of the child. I flatter myself that only a mature art could have dared do this. . . .[69]

Elsewhere she said of her work in this book that she "was striving . . . for a way of writing that was strong, terse, without extraneous adornment, and impeccably true to reality."[70] And she compared her achievements in stylistic effects in several novels when she wrote: ". . . I had felt that *The Sheltered Life* was shot through with scents and colours, that *The Romantic Comedians* was composed of rippling lights, and *They Stooped to Folly* of laughing animation. In the very beginning of *Vein of Iron*, the rhythm tightens and moves swiftly, to the patter of running feet."[71]

V   *Act of Composition*

Ellen Glasgow composed most of her novels on a typewriter in the solitude of her upstairs study at her home in Richmond. She came to believe that she could work nowhere else; actually, she wrote part of *Life and Gabriella* in New York City. She could not dictate: "How I envied . . . those fortunate writers who had learned to dictate! But I had never been able to write except behind a locked door, alone in a room."[72] She was accustomed to make "three separate drafts of a novel: the original sketch, very rapidly tossed together, for balance of structure, vitality of characterization, and in the effort to capture and hold a sustaining mood; the second draft for the sake of atmosphere and the arrangement of scene and detail; and, then, the final writing in a vain search for an austere perfection of style."[73]

Her state of mind and soul during the composition of a novel she liked to call a "state of total immersion." She usually required two years for the first draft of a book and another year for its completion. "All this time," she said, "the imaginary setting becomes the native country of my mind, and the characters are seldom out of my thoughts. I live with them day and night; they are more real to me than acquaintances in the flesh."[74]

She was emphatic concerning the necessity of running down precisely the right word for every situation. But it was in the revision of her work that she found the greatest pleasure. She wrote: ". . . it is the act of scrupulous revision (the endless pruning and trimming for the sake of a valid and flexible prose style) that provides the writer's best solace even while it makes drudgery."[75]

Ellen Glasgow had some advice for other writers of fiction which also tells a good deal about the novelist herself. She wrote:

> . . . Learn the technique of writing, and having learned it thoroughly, try to forget it. Study the principles of construction, the value of continuity, the arrangement of masses, the consistent point of view, the revealing episode, the careful handling of detail, and the fatal pitfalls of dialogue. Then, having mastered, if possible, every rule of thumb, dismiss it into the labyrinth of the memory. Leave it there to make its own signals and flash its own warnings.[76]

A paragraph which Ellen Glasgow wrote shortly after finishing *The Sheltered Life* brings together much that was of great importance to her. She wrote to Daniel Longwell:

> Will anyone suspect, I wonder, that I am writing again, not of Southern nature, but of human nature, that I am writing, not of Southern characteristics (whatever that may mean!), but of the springs of human conduct and the common heritage of mankind? Will anyone even begin to suspect that always, whether I wrote social history or fiction, I was treating the South as a part of the world, that I was concerned neither with a failing system nor with class-consciousness (to which I am profoundly indifferent), but with universal experience? I have included the Southern scene, it is true; I have tried to be accurate in detail, to achieve external verisimilitude; and yet the meaning of my work has never been on the surface. To me, the novel is experience illuminated by the imagination; and by the word "experience" I am trying to convey something more than an attitude or a gesture. In *The Sheltered Life,* as in *Barren Ground,* my idea has been to give the scene an added dimension, a universal rhythm, deeper than any material surface. Beneath the lights and the shadows, there is the spirit of place; beneath the region, there is the whole movement of life. Chekhov has used this motive perfectly in *The Three Sisters.* Many plays and most novels of imaginative reality have touched or suggested it. To me, the Southern landscape contains this living quality, this depth of mood, and all that is needed is the true insight of the novelist.[77]

CHAPTER *3*

Apprentice to the Craft

I *The Descendant*

*T*HE DESCENDANT, Ellen Glasgow's first novel, which was published in 1897, shows her concern with material she treated more effectively later. An apprentice novel, it evinces in tone and in substance insights that promised successful writing. Though readers in 1897 could not have realized this, the book clearly expresses the author's anguish of soul and her rebellion.

The story concerns Michael Akershem, bastard son of a "poor white" mother and of a Virginia aristocrat, who obtains a slight education and then escapes to New York from the humiliation of his Virginia foster home. In New York he rises to importance as editor of a reform journal; meets and lives with Rachel Gavin, a young Southern painter, but becomes estranged from her; and, after being taunted with treason to the reform movement, kills the young assistant who deeply admires him. He serves part of his prison term and leaves, broken in health, to return to the arms of the now successful Rachel and, presumably, to an early death.

Ellen Glasgow put much of herself into both Michael and Rachel. She may have thought of her own education when she wrote of Michael, "Self-taught he was, and self-made he would be."[1] Both Michael and Rachel she endows with her loneliness and her creative interests. Many didactic passages show her speaking of the "New Woman" and other matters which interested her. Michael's account of his early reading and his subscription to the Humboldt Library parallel the author's study in science and political economy and the subscription to the Mercantile Library she received from Cary and Walter McCormack. Rachel's outraged "I always did hate to kiss men!"[2] when Michael kisses her impulsively suggests Ellen Glasgow's admitted dislike of being touched, her implied rejection of physical love-making.

The novel contains many unassimilated ideas drawn from Ellen Glasgow's reading in the biological and social sciences and in philosophy: the emphasis upon the significance of heredity and environment, the deterministic view of biological and social problems, and the pessimistic tone. These ideas, to have been effective in the novel, should have been depicted through action and character development. Instead, the novelist relied too much upon description, narration, and philosophical commentary. Although much of this comment is pertinent, witty, and epigrammatic, it is not an effective substitute for dramatic projection of character.

The chapters most wholly alive are those depicting the child Michael Akershem. In these pages Ellen Glasgow endowed her central figure and those around him with a clarity which the last part of the novel lacks. Michael longs for affection and understanding in the bleak home of the lower-class farmer who shelters him. These opening pages of *The Descendant*, before the author hurries Michael off to New York, are not only the most effective in the book but anticipate her treatment of such people and scenes in *The Voice of the People*, her third novel.

In the remainder of the book, Ellen Glasgow treated material which she did not imagine clearly; her observation of life among artists and writers was too limited. Once Michael Akershem leaves the Virginia woods and fields, a curtain falls between him and the reader; and Rachel Gavin, who had departed from Virginia in a spirit of rebellion, is not sufficiently explored to be entirely believable. Her distinction as an artist, like Akershem's as a writer, must be accepted as an assertion of the novelist. Emotional upheaval and physical violence are too often fortuitous rather than inevitable; and in this respect, the novel suggests unassimilated influences upon the writer from Balzac and Zola as well as from Scott and Hardy.

Ellen Glasgow did not, of course, exhibit mastery of English prose in her first novel; but she did reveal an awareness of the possibilities of language and a desire to use it effectively. *The Descendant* begins with a scene such as she often used to introduce her characters: the person is caught and viewed in natural surroundings—often by a roadside or walking along a road.[3] In the opening chapter of *The Descendant,* she wrote:

The child sat upon the roadside. A stiff wind was rising westward, blowing over stretches of meadowland that had long since run to waste, a scarlet tangle of sumac and sassafras. In the remote West, from whose heart the wind had risen, the death-bed of the Sun showed bloody after the carnage, and nearer at hand naked branches of poplar and sycamore were silhouetted against the shattered horizon, like skeletons of human arms that had withered in the wrath of God.[4]

Clearly her imagery of violent death and decay is overdone. Yet despite rhetorical straining, the paragraph has effectiveness in suggesting anger and violence as well as the waste and decay inherent in untamed nature. Ellen Glasgow was rebelling intellectually and emotionally against the unrealistic, sentimental fiction with which she had been surfeited, but she had not learned how to give adequate aesthetic expression to her rebellion. In this novel she often slipped, therefore, into unmeaning rhetoric, purple passages, and melodramatic posturing. She relied on the repetition of phrases or descriptive characteristics without always making clear their importance.

Her idiom also betrays her dependence upon her reading, her lack of close observation. Such expressions as "Farmer" Watkins (in the mouth of the little boy), "purpling moors" (there are moors in Britain but not in Virginia), and "leader" (for "editorial") have an unnatural quality.

The Descendant lacks humor; its irony has a sardonic cast. Occasionally, however, there are shafts of the wit seasoned with malice characteristic of the later Ellen Glasgow, as in this passage: "I like interesting people better," she said, "but I feel sorrier for the bores. There are so many of them, you know, and they must have such a tiresome time among themselves."[5] Yet most of the barbed thrusts, though epigrammatic, are rarely so sparkling as in subsequent books. One passage suggests an echo of Oscar Wilde, though it is doubtful that Ellen Glasgow had read *The Importance of Being Earnest* when she wrote, "Oh, nobody behaves nowadays, it is not good form; we leave that to the lower classes. . . ."[6]

In spite of shortcomings, *The Descendant* was a commendable first novel. It possessed a vitality which made it readable, and the people in it live as they had lived for the author. Though we may not always understand them completely, we are aware of them as human beings. To have created this illusion of life was a distinction for a young writer.

II *Phases of an Inferior Planet*

Phases of an Inferior Planet (1898), Ellen Glasgow's second novel, is also a story of New York in the latter nineteenth century. Anthony Algarcife—a young scientist-philosopher of powerful passions and rebellious mind—meets, loves, and marries Marianna Musin, a youthful aspirant to operatic fame with more ambition than voice. Algarcife's views favoring "free love" and his outspoken discussion of sex and marriage lead to his dismissal from his teaching post in a girls' college, and he is reduced to hack writing to support himself and Marianna. After the birth of a daughter, Isolde, they are forced to move into slum quarters, and there the infant dies. In desperate poverty they become estranged; and, when Marianna receives a singing offer, she accepts and leaves.

Algarcife, who sinks into poverty and despair, is rescued by an old friend, Father Speares, a "high church" Episcopal priest. Eight years later Algarcife is Father Speares's successor and one of New York's most powerful ministers. Marianna, meanwhile, has lost her singing voice; made a loveless marriage with a wealthy young Englishman; and, broken in health, returned to New York. When she meets Algarcife, she assures him that she loves him, and he resolves to give up his ministry to go to live with her in poverty on a small farm which he conveniently owns in Virginia. Marianna, however, becomes ill; she dies—appropriately—in Algarcife's arms. Algarcife, really an atheist who has entered the Episcopal priesthood only out of gratitude to Father Speares, is interrupted as he is about to commit suicide; he then goes off to intercede in a strike.

In *Phases of an Inferior Planet* Ellen Glasgow wrote of rebellion against convention and personal difficulties. She again brought her central characters from Virginia to New York. In this novel, however, Virginia is one of the places heard about but never seen, and the Southern backgrounds of the characters count for nothing.

Ellen Glasgow is less convincing as a novelist and as an intellectual rebel in *Phases of an Inferior Planet* than in *The Descendant*. Marianna's musical involvement is asserted, not shown. She represents art, as Algarcife represents science and a new philosophy; both stand for a revolt against convention in morals and beliefs. Despite her attempts to dramatize rebellion, the effect is theatrical and melodramatic. Marianna is at first the ingenue and later the lady of the camellias. Algarcife is more a Byronic figure than the central character in a drama of intellectual and spiritual revolt. His intellectual brilliance is not clearly demonstrated, and his power over his parishioners derives from histrionics rather than spiritual force, from a spellbinding personality rather than from a soul. Ellen Glasgow makes it clear that Algarcife has become a priest as his way of repaying Father Speares. He is, then, a hypocrite and a liar. Yet the author does not take this into account in her characterization. The last half of the book is much too contrived.

CHAPTER 4

Virginia in Fiction: Ante-Bellum, Bellum, and Post-Bellum

E LLEN GLASGOW in her first books sought expression for confused feelings and thoughts born of a frustrated childhood and youth and of wide but poorly organized reading. She believed herself in revolt, but she was uncertain of the nature of her rebellion. In *The Voice of the People* (1900), she turned from New York, which she knew slightly, to Virginia and to the characters which belonged to the country of her mind. She determined to celebrate both the new and the old but to look forward to an arriving, living culture rather than back upon a departed South. With this novel she began her Virginia social history in the form of fiction.

I *The Voice of the People*

The Voice of the People tells of life in Virginia from 1870 to 1898 during Reconstruction and the time of the new political developments in the Commonwealth. Nicholas Burr, son of a poor-white "peanut farmer," lives near Kingsborough (Williamsburg) in the Tidewater. With the aid of Judge Bassett, he obtains an education and some legal training. Despite their difference in social status, Nick wins the love of Eugenia Battle, daughter of General Battle whose plantation adjoins the Burr farm. But his hopes of marriage are crushed when Eugenia believes the rumors about his having seduced the daughter of a village storekeeper. The girl and her father clear Nick of all complicity. The real seducer is Bernard Battle, Eugenia's worthless brother.

Nicholas Burr, who becomes an important figure in Virginia politics, is one of the men of the lower class advancing to power in the "New South." His strongest rival is Dudley Webb, young aristocrat and husband of Eugenia. Both men seek the gubernatorial nomination. Nick Burr's forthright defense of Webb against slander captures the imagination of convention delegates; they name Burr as their candidate, and he is elected governor. He fights for honesty in government, even though it endangers his obtaining the senatorial nomination. On the day before the primary election, he goes to Kingsborough. That night a mob comes to lynch a Negro being held for trial. As Nick Burr tries to dissuade them, he is killed by a shot from one of the mob.

In *The Voice of the People* Ellen Glasgow portrayed the complicated social relationships of planter aristocracy, poor-white farmers, village lower middle class, and Negroes in a pattern woven by the traditional and the new in Virginia society, when men from the "lower orders" were entering politics. She knew that caste was a reality in the lives of most Americans, especially Virginians. Although earlier Southern literature assumed that the population was composed of aristocrats and Negroes, she knew that the small farmers and the small town merchants and artisans contributed importantly to Virginia life. She desired to write truthfully of the life lived around her, and she recognized that truthful portrayal must include the lives of all classes.

The actualities stand forth vividly in character and action. The land of the Burrs and the Battles joined; but the social gulf between the poor-white family of ineffectual Amos Burr, small farmer and former overseer, and that of General Thomas Battle, planter-aristocrat, might have seemed broad, deep and impassable to their neighbors. The Negroes exhibited class feeling even more strongly than did their masters. House servants considered themselves infinitely superior to field hands, and both despised the poor whites. That overseers, such as Amos Burr, were often drawn from the ranks of such people probably accounts for this attitude. Yet these Negroes were not harsh or hate-filled; the older Battle Negroes could be kind to little Nick Burr while at the same time they disapproved of his association with the Battle children.

Not all the aristocrats were unaware of change. Judge Bassett recognized the worth of Nick Burr and made it possible for him first to study with his son's tutor and then to study law. Other aristocrats found it necessary to work closely with some of the "new men" if they wished to advance their own political ambitions. A "new man" such as Major Rann represents the unprincipled, vulgar element rising to power. Many persons of the "old school" in the South could, of course, never change their emotional pattern; for example, Mrs. Webb objected to having Dudley study in the same class with Nick Burr; she could never be reconciled to the changed situation. And General Battle, although he liked Nick as a person, could never think of his practicing law; for, to the General, the bar was a profession only for gentlemen. Even Eugenia, who thought that she had no feeling for class, momentarily believed that Nick was guilty of the seduction of the village storekeeper's daughter and condemned him. Nick bitterly ended their relationship.

Ellen Glasgow, who was interested in the results of political activity, was to treat Virginia politics in four other novels (*The Miller of Old Church, The Ancient Law, The Builders,* and *One Man in His Time*); but she never succeeded in moving inside the political arena to an understanding of the intricacies of political action. Where impressions could serve her in *The Voice of the People,* she was successful. Her portrayal of a Virginia nominating convention as a kind of circus is vivid, lively, and valid. We see, hear, and smell the delegates. Yet neither in this episode nor in the scenes in the Capitol and the Governor's Mansion in Richmond could she create an awareness of issues and political forces at work.

Some of the characterization is excellent in *The Voice of the People.* Marthy Burr is one of a gallery of accurate studies of women of the poorer white class. She is thoroughly alive in the hard work and anxiety of a life which offered little else to women of her situation. She finds one reward: her love for her stepson Nick. Ellen Glasgow had an eye and an ear for women such as Marthy. We know her as soon as we hear her rasping, tormented voice in her kitchen, just as we recognize her years later when she comes to Richmond to visit Nick, now the governor, and warns him to be careful with her basket because of the fresh eggs it contains.

Comparable to Marthy Burr's portrait is that of Miss Chris, General Battle's sister, who runs his household. Her functions are similar to those of Mrs. Burr, and she, too, is thoroughly alive in her activities about the house and in her relations to her brother and his children. Less individuals than representatives of their class are Mrs. Webb, the General, and the Judge. They are not "flat" characters, but they lack the individuality of Marthy Burr and Miss Chris. Nick Burr's involvement in social and political meaning hinders his ever appearing just as himself. Dudley Webb and Eugenia Battle are rarely more than just young aristocrats. Aunt Griselda, however, anticipates such later characterizations of embittered spinsters as Miss Kesiah in *The Miller of Old Church*. Her story also dramatizes an extreme form of Southern hospitality: Miss Griselda had come to "Battle Hall" many years before, ostensibly as a guest for a few days; she had unpacked her trunks, settled into the best bedroom, and there she remained. But she was still a guest and had to be so treated!

Next to her characterization, Ellen Glasgow's evocation of setting is the outstanding feature of *The Voice of the People*. Kingsborough is a sleepy county seat, no longer the important center which it had been when it was the capital of colonial Virginia. It serves as an effective stage for the rise of Nick Burr, the new man of the common people who sees his model in Thomas Jefferson. Richmond serves very well as a stage for political scenes, though the treatment in this novel offers little that is essentially characteristic of post-bellum Richmond.

One may object that many of the descriptions of the Virginia countryside in this, as in most of the earlier Glasgow novels, are reminiscent of the methods of Scott and Hardy upon whom the youthful American modeled her work. Yet in *The Voice of the People* the emphasis upon regional atmosphere is justified. The manner of life upon the land is significant for the reader's understanding of the lives of the people. Later Ellen Glasgow learned to use nature more subtly. Even now she was able to draw upon nature to underline effectively the minds and spirits of her characters.

Ellen Glasgow notably improved her style in *The Voice of the People*. Her descriptions are lively and evocative; her narration carries the reader with it. Now and then appear touches of the epigrammatic observation and the ironic thrust characteristic of her best work. Only now and then, however, as in the ironic lines which etch the figure of Mrs. Webb, does Ellen Glasgow touch character and scene with the note of satire. She is at her best when she records the speech of the uneducated village and country white people and the plantation Negroes.

The Voice of the People marked Ellen Glasgow's advance from apprentice writer to professional novelist. Her personal elements are still evident, but her emotional and intellectual stress is no longer so obvious.

II *The Battle-Ground*

The Battle-Ground (1902) is Ellen Glasgow's Civil War novel. Although she did not consider the book essentially romantic, she knew that a truthful account of life in wartime Virginia must be written with romance in mind. She did not intend, however, to perpetuate romantic illusion in still another sentimental narrative justifying the Confederacy. If she wrote of Virginia caught up in a final chivalric gesture, she was keenly aware of the other elements which constituted the reality of the Civil War. She showed the charm and grace of prewar aristocratic existence, but she also depicted the less attractive actualities of that culture and the realities of a society which included those who were neither aristocrats nor slaves.

The Battle-Ground tells of the Lightfoots of "Chericoke" in the Shenandoah Valley and the Amblers of "Uplands"; of Dan Montjoy, Major Lightfoot's grandson, and of Champe Lightfoot, the Major's nephew; of the lives of Betty and Virginia Ambler in the decade before the war; and what the war meant to these Virginians. Dan and Champe fall in love with the Ambler girls; at first Dan with Virginia and Champe with Betty. Dark-haired Virginia, the perfection of ante-bellum Southern beauty, wins the admiration of all the gentlemen. Betty, red-haired and high spirited, has loved Dan since first he appeared, hungry and cold, on his way to "Chericoke." Much of the first half of the book, however, is devoted to interpretation of the life that prevailed among ladies and gentlemen in ante-bellum Virginia.

Shortly before war breaks, Dan and the irascible Major quarrel, and Dan leaves home. When war comes, he serves as a gentleman private in Jackson's "foot cavalry" and survives the four years' struggle. When the war ends, Governor Ambler is dead of a battle wound, Virginia, who had married Jack Morson, is dead, and "Chericoke" has been burned. Dan returns to his grandparents, who are living in the overseer's cottage, and to Betty, whom he had learned long ago to love.

Ellen Glasgow's Civil War story is superior to many of the books which have celebrated that conflict. The novel is not just another fictional treatise justifying the "Lost Cause." The characters are real people rather than costumed figures. The author eschewed the already well-worn plot of the handsome Yankee officer who falls in love with the Southern maiden. Instead she created a romantic narrative which has meaning in the total impact of her book. Largely absent is the moonlight and magnolia nonsense of many Southern romances; *The Battle-Ground* provides more snow and ice than blossoms, and the moonlight often shines upon frozen land. Ellen Glasgow knew that romance was of the essence of her story, but she knew also that it must be a romance true to the people and times of which she wrote, not something superimposed.

For readers familiar with some of the recent Civil War novels, *The Battle-Ground* may seem dated and even a bit tame. It stood, however, in startling contrast to most of the Civil War stories which had preceded it. It is infinitely superior to the extravagances of John Esten Cooke's *Surry of Eagle's Nest* and *Mohun* or to the gentle sentimentalities of Thomas Nelson Page. Where Cooke created museum knights without armor riding about Virginia fields and where Page idealized most of the humanity out of his characters, Ellen Glasgow created people who, while representative, are individual human beings and not simply clotheshorses. Her people are persons rather than mere personalities. She realized that idealism, cruelty, and the horror of war must be mingled if her story of that conflict were to convey truth; but she was not wholly successful in doing all that she might have done in these respects. She was able to imagine the problems and sufferings of the noncombatants far more clearly than those of the soldiers.[1] Her scenes in camp, on the march, and in battle are lively; but they lack the authentic tone of her accounts of life in Richmond or on the Valley farms during the war. *The Battle-Ground* is generally rather than specifically historical in its treatment of life in the Valley of Virginia and of the Civil War experience. In later work Ellen Glasgow gave the feeling of a particular time and place; in this book she did little more than assert their existence. The story, nevertheless, compares well with such admired Civil War novels as Stark Young's *So Red the Rose* and Margaret Mitchell's *Gone with the Wind.*

The people of *The Battle-Ground* are representative of several classes of Southerners. Not only are the ladies and gentlemen present but so are those who had been so largely neglected in Southern fiction: the poor whites, worthy and villainous; and the free Negro as well as the slave. Of the poor whites, Pinetop, the tall soldier from the Blue Ridge Mountains, stands out. The friendship of Pinetop and Dan emphasizes the democracy of the ranks. Pinetop's illiteracy underlines the pathetic situation of the intelligent poor white in an aristocratic society in which education had long been the prerogative of the gentleman.

Some characters are little more than shadows. Virginia Ambler is a gentle and lovely but just a bit insipid Southern beauty. Miss Lydia hardly lives away from her flowers and her small gentilities. Mrs. Ambler is a wraithlike Virginia lady never very clearly seen except in relation to her husband. Major Lightfoot is the type of fire-eating ex-soldier who hates the North and urges secession. His neighbor, Governor Ambler, is more vividly depicted; for Ellen Glasgow saw in him the tragedy of the Southern gentleman who hated war and secession, who loved Virginia and the Union, yet who felt obligated to fight for his state and the South when the war came and who, in final irony, lost his life in a war he had done all in his power to prevent.

Because she gave little attention to structure in her early novels, Ellen Glasgow neglected point of view as a fictional device. In *The Battle-Ground* she used the point of view of the omniscient author and shifted the emphasis freely from one character to another. She was still learning her craft, and she made relatively little advance in matters of style beyond her work in *The Voice of the People*. Her language for narrative and descriptive purposes is usually effective and thoroughly readable in *The Battle-Ground*, but it is no more than this.

The Battle-Ground has merit and is still, in a day of brutal war fiction, a rewarding novel. When it appeared in 1902, it was an innovation in Civil War literature; it was a novel that admitted the romantic nature of that unfortunate conflict yet offered a stern observation of its unromantic aspects.

III   *The Deliverance*

The Deliverance (1904) was superior to anything Ellen Glasgow had written before, and it compares well with much of her later fiction. It covers a period following the bitterest events of the Reconstruction, when the social structure of Virginia had been disrupted violently by the war and its aftermath, and the ladies and gentlemen of the aristocracy were exhausted not only economically but often spiritually. The novel focuses upon the aristocratic Blakes and the lowborn Fletchers of 1878, some ten years after the Blakes have been dispossessed of "Blake Hall" by their former overseer, Bill Fletcher. The family had been forced to move into an overseer's cottage, and there young Christopher and his twin sister, Lila, had grown up deprived of their birthright. There Cynthia, the older sister, slaves at keeping the family together while Christopher ekes out a living. There, too, live old Mrs. Blake, blind and deluded, and Uncle Tucker Corbin, one of Ellen Glasgow's gallery of the civilized who are maimed in body but thriving in spirit.

Christopher Blake's existence is shaped by his hatred for Bill Fletcher. The Fletcher ménage comprises the old man, his sister Miss Sadie, his granddaughter, Maria, and his weakling grandson, Will. Inadvertently, Christopher saves Will's life and wins his friendship. Realizing that the boy is the old man's vulnerable spot, Christopher deliberately leads the boy into drunkenness and wild escapades which cause a break between old Fletcher and his grandson. Will's foolish marriage to Molly Peterkin, the promiscuous daughter of a poor white, infuriates Fletcher; he gives the boy a worn-out little farm in the neighborhood and orders him never to appear at "Blake Hall."

Maria Fletcher, after an unhappy marriage, returns to "Blake Hall." She and Christopher meet again, and, in spite of his hatred of all things Fletcher, he cannot resist her. The poison Christopher has spread between Will and his grandfather brings on a final clash. When the desperate young alcoholic kills old Fletcher, Christopher Blake not only helps the demoralized boy to leave the country but assumes the blame for the murder. After three years of health-destroying prison confinement, Christopher is pardoned when word comes from Will in Europe telling the truth about Fletcher's death. Liberated from prison and supposedly from his hatred, Christopher returns to the land and the love of Maria.

Christopher Blake believed that during the long period of his father's illness, when he himself had been a small child, Bill Fletcher had milked the Blake fortune and acquired the seven thousand dollars with which he had purchased "Blake Hall" and its land when they were very suddenly sold at auction. Although Christopher could never prove Fletcher guilty, he never doubted his guilt.

Socially, too, the feeling of the Blakes toward Fletcher is valid. As the agent of the owner in the operation of slavery on the plantation, the slave overseer incurred, perhaps unjustly, an opprobrium comparable to that of a hangman: his services were considered necessary but he himself was despised. In the Virginia social scale, he was far below his planter employer and most of his white neighbors, whether middle-class yeoman farmers or even the poorer white farmers; but he might eventually rise above many of his neighbors in all except esteem. Such men might live for the pleasure derived from the simple ownership of money. Coarse, vulgar, ignorant, yet shrewd, Bill Fletcher had devoted himself with single-minded urgency to making himself "master" of "Blake Hall."

That he cannot, in fact, become master simply by controlling the land and living in the house is forever a frustration to Fletcher. He sees that the poverty-stricken Blakes still receive the homage of white and black alike: the former Blake servants hurry to open a gate for Christopher, but they ignore Fletcher's shouted demands for the same service; the Negroes work in Christopher's tobacco fields when he needs them, but they cannot be found when Fletcher seeks them in a busy season. Even the poorer white farmers and the storekeeper respect the Blakes but despise the Fletchers.

Of the Fletchers, Maria is least a Fletcher. A figure of romance in this novel rather than a member of the Fletcher household, she is an alien spirit in a "Blake Hall" presided over by old Bill and Miss Sadie. When she returns from her humiliating marriage, she is chastened, sad, and yet determined to stand up to her irascible old grandfather and to bring some decency into "Blake Hall"; and the old man comes to respect her. Will Fletcher is always a victim, the pawn of his grandfather's ambition and of Christopher Blake's hatred. Although it is obvious that he is a device and that his fictional purpose is to serve in the working out of the destinies of the two men between whom he is caught, he is a thoroughly believable figure.

The Blakes are even more carefully depicted than the hated Fletchers. Mrs. Blake, paralyzed and blind, is sustained in her belief in a departed gentility through the drudgery of Christopher and Cynthia and the conspiracy of her family to perpetuate a lie. In her physical blindness the old lady is a symbol of the attitude of intellectual and spiritual evasion in the South—of the "evasive idealism" which Ellen Glasgow frequently attacked throughout her career.

Christopher and Lila, however, find the old codes onerous.

Lila rebels in loving Jim Weatherby, a man of a lower class, and Christopher sympathizes with her; but he withholds his approval because of consideration for their mother. Lila, delicate and protected from hardship by Cynthia, remains a shadowy figure: sentimentally sweet and usually seen in relation to Cynthia, Christopher, or her lover, she is only occasionally brightened by some spark of fire of her own.

Cynthia Blake is a curiously pathetic yet admirable person. She has devoted her life to providing a home for her brother and uncle, to maintaining the dream that someday Lila may realize the life of a lady, and to preserving the illusion of her blind mother. Mrs. Blake's death removes Cynthia's strongest argument for opposing the marriage of Lila and Jim. At the end of the novel Cynthia is pathetically deprived of her motives, although the reader may believe that the happiness of Jim and Lila has brought some softening in her harshness toward the violation of her code. In her twisted fashion Cynthia Blake is a heroic figure as a demonstration of the power of a code of manners enabling its possessor to surmount even the daily living of a lie.

Uncle Tucker Corbin is endowed with riches of spirit which permit him to overcome his disabilities and to find a deep happiness in the small details of his daily life. He is the first of Ellen Glasgow's gallery of civilized men; and, more than an aristocrat by birth and class, he is an aristocrat of the mind and soul. Instead of embittering him, his afflictions have strengthened him. Yet he is neither sentimental, nor blind to suffering. He is no Pollyanna any more than he is a victim of self-pity. Perhaps he is a truly civilized man.

Uncle Tucker, like other of the author's civilized persons, embodies qualities and attitudes which she admired but which, as her autobiography and her letters clearly show, she herself did not possess. The philosophy of Uncle Tucker, comparable in some respects to that of General Archbald in *The Sheltered Life,* of John Fincastle in *Vein of Iron,* or of Asa Timberlake in *In This Our Life,* is not one which Ellen Glasgow ever succeeded in putting into effect in her own life, much as she admired it.

Through Christopher Blake are dramatized the near-tragic effects of hatred as well as the regenerating working of love. His portrait is diffused by his involvement in both the love story and the drama of bitter hatred. It is not impossible that one man may be so involved and yet be shown as capable of the tenderest af-

tection and the bitterest hate; the difficulty is that Christopher
Blake was conceived by the author as the victim and the instrument of inherited hatred and only incidentally as the lover. Christopher's deliberate seduction of Will Fletcher constitutes one of
Ellen Glasgow's more successful creations of tragic action. Young
Blake's awareness of the nature of what he is doing makes the
horror of his deed all the greater. So strong is his hatred depicted
that his regeneration cannot be so convincing as it was meant to
be.

The Negroes in *The Deliverance,* as in the two novels which
preceded it, are still very near their former slave status. Most of
them are "Blake Negroes," former servants of the family who
continued to live in the vicinity of "Blake Hall" after they had
received their freedom. Even though the Blakes have been reduced to penury, these Negroes still regard them as their masters
in all but law.

In this novel Ellen Glasgow showed more emphatically that
not all Virginia rural common folk were alike. Not only were
there people like the Fletchers; there were also respected plain
people such as the Weatherbys. Old Jacob Weatherby had once
been a laborer for the Blakes. Now he and his son were fairly
prosperous tobacco farmers, and Jim had won the love of Lila
Blake. The Weatherbys may remind us of the Burrs in *The Voice
of the People,* but they have moved a few notches higher on the
social and economic scale.

Sol Peterkin, his numerous if shadowy wives, and his sluttish
daughter, Molly, are Southern "poor white trash." In morals, culture, and social status they are much farther below the Weatherbys than the Blakes are above those worthy people. Sol is ignorant
and vulgar. Molly is pathetic and despicable, with the sexual
inclinations of a rabbit. Will Fletcher, in his simple-minded infatuation for her blonde prettiness, doesn't realize what she is; but
the village people know her, and old Bill Fletcher does too.

Somewhere between the Peterkins and the Weatherbys are the
Spades: Tom, the storekeeper, and his domineering wife, Susan.
Mrs. Spade believes inflexibly that if anything is pleasant it is
wrong. She possesses most of the ignorance, prejudice, puritanical
religious distortion, certainty of moral virtue, narrowness, and
shrewdness of her class. Whenever we see her or hear her speaking her mind, we know that we are in the presence of a living
person; she is never simply a type.

Carraway, the lawyer, is part of the social structure of Virginia yet separated from it. He belongs to the lower ranks but has lifted himself above the common folk. He contemplates the situation of the Blakes with mingled pity and scorn. He cannot keep himself from looking up to the Blakes, yet he scorns them with the old antipathy of the hardworking common man for the soft-handed gentleman. Carraway recognizes Fletcher as one of his own people, but he despises him for his meanness and madness.

Ellen Glasgow's evocation of place in *The Deliverance* is excellent. The tobacco fields and all the processes of tobacco culture are brought forcefully to life in relation to the people. Into this novel the author wove the activity of the tobacco farmer from the back-breaking labor of planting the fields through the tedious, messy work of caring for the growing plants and the various processes of cutting, curing, and sorting the leaves. She also created interesting ironies in Christopher's dislike of tobacco coupled with his skill in its culture and his mother's attitude toward the use of tobacco: a cigar was a gentleman's smoke; a pipe was intolerable, and, of course, chewing and dipping snuff were beyond her consideration.

Readers of *The Deliverance* may note one rather peculiar circumstance: the absence of other aristocrats. The Blakes overshadow all the other persons of the story. We might suppose, however, that in this community lived other persons in comparable circumstances, yet no other aristocrats are mentioned. Economy of narrative and dramatic structure in this novel may have suggested the restriction of the aristocrats to one family.

Ellen Glasgow showed improvement in her craft in *The Deliverance*. Structural relations of character, scene, and action are more effectively developed; there is more awareness of fictional techniques. The author uses Carraway to control point of view and occasionally as a "chorus" voice through whom she comments on people and action or suggests the direction of thought. Now and then some of the common folk or the Negroes function in the same way.

The essay about *The Deliverance* in *A Certain Measure* is notable for Ellen Glasgow's observation that "in this novel, as in *Barren Ground,* [she had] tried to depict that land as a living personality, and to portray its characteristics in the central figures."[2] She commented upon the "epic quality of [the] atmosphere" and about her views of environmental determinism.[3]

She also provided an interesting observation about the characters with respect to Uncle Tucker, "a civilized soul in a world which, by and large, is not, and may not ever become, civilized";[4] and she related Mrs. Blake, once a Southern belle, to other portraits of Southern beauties such as Mrs. Birdsong of *The Sheltered Life* and Mrs. Dalrymple of *They Stooped to Folly*. She remarked that even in her youth she had "liked to write of old people, because the old alone have finality."[5]

IV *Inferior Works*

The Freeman and Other Poems (1902) is of relatively little importance. Ellen Glasgow had written verse from childhood; she wrote a few poems occasionally in the years following the publication of this collection. But it is clear that verse was not her creative medium. Although she believed that her poems were daring, they offer little that is original or unusual. Most of them may be compared with the more gloomy verse of the turn of the century or with the rhetorical declarations of such late Victorian English poets as William Ernest Henley, author of "Invictus." The epigraph at the head of the volume—"Hope is a slave. Despair is a freeman."—sets the mood for the verses which follow. Yet Ellen Glasgow's proclamation of freedom through despair, echoed from time to time in her novels, sounds windily rhetorical against the actuality of her life, her struggle to attain such spiritual freedom, and her ultimate failure to win real peace of mind. Perhaps in her novel, as in these verses, the novelist portrayed the achievement of a spiritual peace which she sought unavailingly in her own life. These and other poems show clearly that Ellen Glasgow could not write enduring verse. She could never capture a clear understanding of the poet's craft.

The Wheel of Life (1906) and *The Ancient Law* (1908) are inferior to most of Ellen Glasgow's other fiction and represent interruptions in her development as a novelist. Neither merits extended examination, and in later years even the author repudiated both books. In *The Wheel of Life,* Ellen Glasgow used New York City as her setting and a group of wealthy, eccentric or bohemian individuals as her characters. In most respects the book is a throw-back in material and tone to her apprentice volumes. Nor is it greatly superior to them in style and development. Apparently, she drew too directly upon the experiences of her own love affair with the man she called Gerald. Her character Laura Wilde probably embodies much that she thought true of own personality, but it is not clear that Gerald is represented in any of the three men importantly involved in the story. In tone the book varies from the novel of manners to something very near domestic sentimentality and melodrama. Although this novel might be compared with such books by Edith Wharton as *The House of Mirth* or *The Age of Innocence*, the comparison would be overwhelmingly to Mrs. Wharton's advantage. Edith Wharton possessed her New York scene and people; Ellen Glasgow was forever only a visitor to the metropolis.

In *The Ancient Law* Ellen Glasgow returned to Virginia for scene and characters. Yet the novel is a failure despite some virtues. It is interesting, often stimulating, but, at the same time, an irritating, frustrating work. Perhaps the novelist attempted to crowd too much into this book. For in it are several varieties of Southern aristocrat: the proud but poor, the relatively wealthy but spiritually dead, and the ideally proud but perspicacious and courageous individual. Through these pages move several degrees of lower-class white Southerners, from the fairly-well-to-do to the ignorant, starving, and demoralized.

Apparently Ellen Glasgow never saw clearly her way to shaping her material into a natural and inevitable pattern in this book. She fell back upon eccentricity and melodramatic stereotype for characterization and action. Her central character, Daniel Ordway, is too virtuous and long-suffering to be endured. And her use of coincidence is obviously a device to enable her to keep her story moving toward some eventual end. Only Emily Brooke, who anticipates such interesting Glasgow characters as Dorinda of *Barren Ground* or Ada of *Vein of Iron,* and Ordway's cold wife, who anticipates some of Ellen Glasgow's later repulsive if pitiful females, redeem the book to some extent. Jasper Trend, the never-too-clearly-seen cotton-mill owner, symbolizes the advent of financial vultures in the South, such persons as William Faulkner would portray later in his infamous Snopes clan. Later, too, Ellen Glasgow would develop leaders of industry and commerce more vividly delineated, such as old Cyrus Treadwell of *Virginia* and old Mr. Fitzroy of *In This Our Life.* In spite of interesting parts, *The Ancient Law* fails as a work of art.

CHAPTER 5

Plain People in Town and Country

THE TWO NOVELS published in 1909 and 1911, *The Romance of a Plain Man* and *The Miller of Old Church*, represent the beginning of a period of more rewarding productivity in Ellen Glasgow's career. *Virginia* and *Life and Gabriella*, the two novels which follow them, showed the novelist maintaining her higher standard. After that she experienced a falling off in creative energy and wrote with less effectiveness in the works published between *Life and Gabriella* in 1916 and the appearance of *Barren Ground* in 1925.

The Romance of a Plain Man and *The Miller of Old Church* may be read as companion studies of the changing status of Virginia common folk and aristocrats in the urban and rural areas of the Commonwealth. As a result of Ellen Glasgow's clearer view of her Virginia neighbors and their ways, these novels come to grips with the personalities of Virginia people without having less universal pertinence.

I *The Romance of a Plain Man*

In *The Romance of a Plain Man* Ben Starr narrates the story of his rise from poverty-blighted commonness to wealth, distinction, and a measure of social acceptance in the Richmond of 1875 to 1910. Determined to remove his taint of commonness—of which he had first become conscious at seven when so labeled by little Sally Mickleborough, aristocrat—Ben Starr moves from grocery delivery boy to a job in a tobacco factory and then to a place as assistant to the president of the Great South Midland and Atlantic Railroad. As old General Bolingbroke's assistant, Ben becomes the white-haired boy of Richmond commercial activities. Eventually, but rather rapidly, he rises to the presidency of a Richmond bank and is soon a very wealthy man. This rise in the business world parallels Starr's ascent in Richmond social circles which reaches a high point with his marriage to Sally Mickleborough, the niece of the proudly aristocratic Misses Matoaca and Mitty Bland and the same girl who, when small, had called Ben "common."

More and more Ben's business affairs consume his time, and he no longer gives his wife the devotion she requires; but, when financial panic strikes and Ben's fortune is swept away, Sally watches over him in his illness. Gradually he recovers his health. Soon, however, he becomes more and more absorbed in his business affairs, and again Sally seeks an outlet for her unhappiness in frivolous amusements. Ultimately, her association with George Bolingbroke, the General's nephew who has long loved her, threatens to become an open scandal. Ben Starr comes to his senses just in time to prevent the ruin of their marriage; he now realizes that he cannot devote all his time to making money and that the love of his wife cannot be bought by showering her with what money will purchase. When he is offered the presidency of the Great South Midland and Atlantic Railroad upon the retirement of General Bolingbroke, he refuses the offer although it represents the goal which he has sought all his life. Now he prefers Sally's love to power and increasing wealth.

Much of the characterization in *The Romance of a Plain Man* suggests people encountered in earlier novels: Mrs. Starr, Ben's hard-working mother, reminds one of Marthy Burr in *The Voice of the People*. General Bolingbroke resembles General Battle in that earlier novel, although General Bolingbroke has a force which General Battle never suggests. The aristocrats in *The Romance of a Plain Man* are, of course, brothers and sisters of those in the earlier novels; but they have their own individuality and, in most respects, are more interesting people. In *The Voice of the People*, *The Wheel of Life*, and *The Ancient Law*, the aristocrats often appeared as waxworks curiosities, as representatives of their class instead of unique persons with their own places in life; but in *The Romance of a Plain Man*, as in *The Deliverance*, the ladies and gentleman are not only typical but individual.

The Romance of a Plain Man is heroic romance although the scene is post-bellum Richmond rather than Camelot, the armored steeds are locomotives, the weapons are stocks and bonds, and the lists the stock exchange, the bank, and the coal mine. Read thus, the novel carries a flavor and a meaning which is not evident if it is considered a straightforward, realistic narrative. Ben Starr's "rise" may too closely resemble the upward and onward march to materialistic success of Horatio Alger's heroes. Perhaps there is more than a touch of the Horatian (or is it Algerian?) hero in Ben, his outlook, and his actions. On the other hand, the dime novel of a young man's rise to fame, fortune, and the girl did not possess the ironic overtones and the satiric meanings which *The Romance of a Plain Man* carries on almost every page. We might, therefore, be tempted to call this novel a mock heroic work in prose except for the fact that Ellen Glasgow did not mock, nor do her form and her style represent a mock imitation. There is satire, indeed, but not that of the mock epic.

To achieve a different view of the rising common man, to bring a sharper edge to her satire and the ironies of her action, Ellen Glasgow used a first-person narrator, Ben Starr himself; and she was able to make the first-person narrative method a flexible instrument for her purposes. Certainly, this method compelled her to maintain a consistent point of view and to create a style suitable to the personality and background of Ben Starr. In actual practice—as with such narration in the work of other novelists, especially Henry James—Ellen Glasgow did not always relinquish her own voice or point of view. Frequently, we have difficulty in distinguishing Ben's words from the words and thoughts of his creator.

Ellen Glasgow chose a procedure which enabled her to avoid some of the potential pitfalls of first-person narrative. She wrote the book as if it were the work of a man who had fashioned his use of the English language through his reading of seventeenth- and eighteenth-century English classics—and especially the study of Samuel Johnson's dictionary. She provides an eighteenth-century flavor to the story in the balanced, usually clear prose in which Ben tells of his life. Because Ben is a humorless individual, the book lacks the humorous or the satiric comments which enliven the best of Ellen Glasgow's fiction; but there are ironic overtones in his narrative.

Ben is almost insufferable when he proclaims his achievements as a business wonder boy. (Or was this Ellen Glasgow's notion of the epic boast?) Ben is no snob, and he despises the shallow snobbishness of his young sister, Jessy. Yet Ben's poverty and hard struggle, as well as the materialism central to his character, had shaped a man whose sense of values left much to be desired. He had grown to manhood convinced that greatness resided in the acquisition of money and economic power, for he saw both embodied in General Bolingbroke, his benefactor. Throughout the book Ben struggles with the conflict between his materialistic "values" and his vague realization that there are other values by which one may live. The reader may wonder, however, whether the Ben Starr who has told his story could ever be aware of other than material meanings.

The end of the novel, with Ben Starr's renunciation of his material prize, belongs to the heroic romance that *The Romance of a Plain Man* is. Ben's single-minded pursuit of his prize also brings out an important pattern of meanings and relationships: the comparisons and the contrasts of the common folk and the aristocrats in their attitudes. For Ben Starr, lacking money and inherited social position, only economic power can bring freedom from commonness. Can he ever believe anything else? But for the Misses Mitty and Matoaca Bland, "family" is everything; no material success can change the fact that Ben's father had been a laboring man; and no amount of worthlessness can erase the fact of inherited position for Sally's scamp of a father or for George Bolingbroke, the General's nephew. The General combines the two traditions: he has achieved wealth and power in the hard postwar days, and he prizes his railroad; yet he is no less the aristocrat for all his devotion to money.

In this novel the characters have an added value in that they are clearly relevant to the purposes of the book. If there is a touch of Dickens in the plain people, as well as in the plot, which is reminiscent of *Great Expectations,* this is acceptable. Ben's hard-working, driving mother—who knows nothing but work and the effort to maintain some decency in her home—joins Ellen Glasgow's other plain women: she is a sister in toil, pain, stern opinions and flavorful speech of Marthy Burr and Mrs. Spade. Ben's father is another of Ellen Glasgow's well-meaning but ineffectual poor men.

The aristocrats—the Misses Bland, Dr. Theophilus Pry, General Bolingbroke—present a variety of personalities and attitudes. Miss Matoaca Bland is the more interesting of the two sisters; she horrifies her one-time suitor, the old General, by taking an interest in politics. Indeed, her devotion to her "principles" eventually kills her. Miss Mitty is the unbending lady who can never forgive her niece for marrying "beneath" her nor accept Ben Starr, no matter what he achieves. Dr. Theophilus Pry, Ben Starr's mentor, is delightful and far from the "mollycoddle" his friend the General accuses him of being; he represents the scholar-aristocrat in a time when his values no longer claimed the respect of money and power. A mark of Ben Starr's percipience as a man is his not sharing General Bolingbroke's opinion of the old physician. The younger ladies and gentlemen, especially George Bolingbroke and Bonny Marshall, are more lightly sketched as types of idle, fox-hunting Virginia gentlefolk.

The Romance of a Plain Man is the first novel in which Ellen Glasgow used Richmond as her setting so extensively and in which she drew directly upon childhood memories. Old Richmond, especially the Church Hill section near St. John's Church, is brilliantly suggested in those portions of the novel treating Ben's childhood and, later, Ben's and Sally's residence in the house with the enchanted garden. But it is not only a Richmond of intimate neighborhoods of ladies and gentlemen, such as Ellen Glasgow had known in her childhood, but also one of poorer sections where people such as the Starrs dwelt. Not only did Ellen Glasgow use her recollections of scenes and flavors but she introduced some of her own experience into the novel: the mistreated horses which aroused her hatred of cruelty and inspired her life-long effort against brutality to animals are recalled in the episode when Ben stops a driver from beating his horse and then puts his shoulder against the wheel of the wagon, an "heroic" episode which is a significant turning point in the novel.

Ellen Glasgow was interested in the *effect* of the business struggle on individuals rather than in the details of business activity. Although she never wholly condemns the era of the "Great Barbecue" in this novel, her portrayal of changing post-Civil War times as they were lived in the South spreads no veneer of glamor over the age.

The structure of this novel shows marked improvement over that of preceding books. Character, action, and atmosphere are pertinently related. Only in one important respect does a structural defect appear: the break in sustained movement between Ben's childhood and his early youth. This defect is comparable to the same shortcoming in *The Voice of the People* in which Nick Burr's childhood and manhood belong to different people. In

The Romance of a Plain Man, however, the break in the movement is less noticeable.

The relatively brief essay on *The Romance of a Plain Man* in *A
Certain Measure* concerns the genesis of the novel as it related
especially to the childhood experiences of the author. Ellen Glasgow thought that in her own work she had been neither derivative
nor imitative—a questionable view. She offered a not very convincing defense of the first-person narrative method she had
used: she had told the story that way because that was the way it
had come to her.[1] She also expressed her antipathy to what she
called "the present grotesque revival in Southern fiction. . . ."[2]

II *The Miller of Old Church*

In *The Miller of Old Church* (1911) are present plebeian emer-
gence, aristocratic decadence, and the complexities of a rural
society in transition. *The Romance of a Plain Man* focuses attention upon the economic and social ascent of a plain man in the
commercial and social world of Richmond, but *The Miller of Old
Church* is concerned not only with economic and political change
for the small farmer but with its relation to the changing status
of the rural aristocrat at the close of the century. Both *The Miller
of Old Church* and *The Deliverance* present, therefore, conflicts
between plebeian and aristocrat. In both books the common folk
attempt to improve themselves economically and socially, while
the aristocrats appear in a decadent situation.

The Miller of Old Church is placed in southside Virginia in a
part of the state where "the first settlers were almost entirely
English" and where "the native speech was still tinctured with the
racy flavour of old England."[3] Near the mill, not far from Bottom's
Ordinary, live the Revercombs: Abel, the young miller; Sarah, his
mother; his aged grandparents; his older brother, Abner; his
younger brother, Archie; and Abner's daughter, Blossom. Not far
away at "Jordan's Journey" live the aristocratic Gays: Angela, old
Jonathan Gay's sister-in-law; her son, young Jonathan; and her
old-maid sister, Miss Kesiah. In a cottage nearby live Reuben
Merryweather and his granddaughter, Molly, the illegitimate
child of old Jonathan and of Reuben's daughter, Janet, both now
dead.

Abel Revercomb loves Molly; but, having been dismissed
once too often, he marries ugly, repressed Judy Hatch. After her

grandfather's death, Molly lives with Mrs. Gay and Miss Kesiah; and rumors develop that she may marry young Jonathan Gay, Angela's son. In the meantime Abel Revercomb is rising politically in his part of the state, and his wife Judy longs hopelessly for the love of young Mr. Orlando Mullen, the Episcopal minister. She is broken-hearted when she learns that he plans to leave the community, and when Mr. Mullen's horse runs away with him (with no damage except to his self-esteem), Judy goes into a state of shock and dies after bearing a stillborn child.

When the Gays return to "Jordan's Journey" with Molly, young Jonathan finds the girl increasingly attractive. Because of his mother's supposed delicate health and feelings, Jonathan has, indeed, never revealed his secret marriage to the lovely, if rather dull, Blossom Revercomb. Abner Revercomb long ago had loved Janet Merryweather and had been suspected of killing old Jonathan Gay, Janet's betrayer. Now Abner believes that young Jonathan Gay has seduced his daughter, Blossom. He lies in wait for Gay and shoots him. Young Jonathan dies, without revealing his slayer; now with Judy and Jonathan dead, Abel may woo and win Molly. Upon the death of her son, Angela Gay displays her usual "fortitude," while everyone around her conspires to shield her from the truth. It is clear that actually she knows the truths involved in the lives of the Gays, but she refuses to admit anything unpleasant as possibly relevant to her. Her insidious influence has brought about the death of her brother-in-law and her son.

With a divided emphasis, the structure of *The Miller of Old Church* is much looser than that of *The Romance of a Plain Man*. The reader's attention is directed from common folk to aristocrat and back again; but Molly Merryweather, with her heritage from both classes, weaves the pattern of forces which compose the action. The characters of *The Miller of Old Church* may remind us of the people in Hardy's novels: the common folk, particularly the old people, suggest some of the English peasants in *Under the Greenwood Tree* or *The Mayor of Casterbridge*; the aristocrats sometimes suggest the ladies and gentlemen in *Tess of the D'Urbervilles*.

Ellen Glasgow offered a set of country portraits which surveyed nearly the whole range of personalities among farm and village people in Virginia at the turn of the century. She also struck the Hardy note in the account, at the opening of the novel, of the gathering at Bottom's Ordinary, the village tavern. Betsy Bottom runs the tavern and store to which most of the farm folk in the neighborhood resort. A vigorous, energetic, vulgar woman, she presides over the villagers with a firm hand and a sharp tongue. Among those who frequent Bottom's Ordinary, the most vividly defined are the nonagenerian, Adam Doolittle, and his son, young Adam, a mere youth of some fifty years. Old Adam's pronouncements about all matters lend flavor to the talk; he and the other villagers at the tavern serve as chorus, with Old Adam and Betsy Bottom as chorus leaders.

The Revercombs offer another view of Virginia common people. Ellen Glasgow sketched in Abel a portrait of the young yeoman farmer trying to improve himself and his family economically; to find his place politically in the Commonwealth; and, in the process, to lift himself and his family socially. He is not consciously "social climbing"; however, he begins to attend the Episcopal Church instead of the Presbyterian Church of his mother, certainly a hint of social aspiration in Virginia. Young Revercomb is an idealized figure of the "new" man in Southern rural life at the turn of the century. Endowed by his author with a stature more heroic than that of the rest of his family, he is intellectually, morally and spiritually superior to them. He contrasts to his rather oafish brother Abner, who is almost an unthinking clod on the land—a type Ellen Glasgow had portrayed in Amos Burr in *The Voice of the People* and later depicted in Joshua Oakley in *Barren Ground*. Abel has bought the mill and so added the role of rural entrepreneur to that of farmer, a pattern repeated in Nathan Pedlar of *Barren Ground*; he is beginning to take a hand in local politics and to aspire to election to the legislature; and the reader is allowed to witness Abel at a stump speaking. Because Ellen Glasgow did not make the mistake in this novel she later made in *The Builders*, where she interlards her book with political theory and expostulation, the references to politics remain generalities in spite of the significance of Abel's increasing political influence. In *The Miller of Old Church* Abel is most prominently shown as the frustrated, if ultimately rewarded, lover of Molly Merryweather; hence, his other functions in the novel are only lightly suggested.

Archie Revercomb, the younger brother of Abner and Abel, is the irresponsible, spoiled, fairly bright but unambitious country boy whose main interest is amusing himself. He is selfish, thoughtless, a bit pugnacious, but not actually bad. Archie exhibits the strain of Virginia common people which would waste its energies in pointless activities while Abel and others like him moved. Archie is an early sketch of the worthless country youngster who later appeared more significantly as Dorinda Oakley's brother Rufus in *Barren Ground*.

Blossom Revercomb may have been modeled on Hardy's Tess, but she is far more passive than Tess. Yet she is sufficiently knowing to prevail upon young Jonathan Gay to marry her before she surrenders herself to her love for him. She apparently loves Jonathan Gay passionately, yet she appears to be an almost cow-like personality. Actually, Blossom functions more as a motivating factor in the novel than as a human actor in her own drama.

Sarah Revercomb, the most spicy individual in the miller's household, rules the family with tyranny masked as sacrifice. She is another of Ellen Glasgow's insufferably good, hard-working, sharp-tongued common women who manage to make life a hell for those around them while absolutely certain that they are sacrificing everything for the welfare of others. Sarah glories in her widowhood, bosses Archie until he takes to the fields to escape, and constantly pecks away at Abel until he can scarcely endure her torment. With Abner, her eldest son, Sarah has less influence; for he has withdrawn into his own gloom. With Blossom, Abner's daughter, Sarah lives on fairly equable terms because the girl absorbs her grandmother's scolding the same way she breathes air.

Sarah Revercomb is a voice of a Southern puritanism which once constituted the sustaining "vein of iron" among common folk and in which Ellen Glasgow preserved an inquiring interest. In Sarah, Presbyterianism had bloomed in its less attractive flower. For her, religion is a stern yet stimulating and perversely inspiring source of energy. Her faith is, above all, a means of asserting her superiority over her more liberal neighbors who follow the preaching of the Episcopal rector. If Sarah Revercomb represents Ellen Glasgow's bitter reaction to her father's Calvinism and to what she believed to be an ugliness in its spiritual life even while it was tough and hard, then Orlando Mullen and his Episcopal liberalism stand for her scornful rejection of a shallow, saccharine, snobbish, "superior" substitute.

Reuben Merryweather always appears in an attractive role as

one who has had to endure much, has been cruelly treated by fate, yet has been able to preserve sweetness and a certain mild wisdom despite his troubles. His love for his tormented grand-daughter Molly and hers for him are developed into an excessively idealistic phase of the novel.

Molly Merryweather is throughout the book the center of action. As we have noted, Ellen Glasgow uses the girl as the symbol of a mingling of the aristocratic blood of the Gays and the plebeian blood of the victimized Janet Merryweather; as a result, Molly carries too heavy a burden of meaning. She is a tormented child in mind and emotions sometime after she is a woman in body and desires. She hates not only the Gay who be-trayed her mother but all men because of that betrayal, and she thinks she must punish the male animal for her mother's suffer-ing. Yet her hate cannot, ultimately, survive against the forces of affection and sexual desire. All through the novel, the battle of these forces continues until Molly permits her love for the miller to prevail. Because Molly is a symbol as well as a person, her characterization also suffers a confusion of direction. Her alternating moods of hate and love, scorn and affection, are undoubtedly human. Yet she does not always appear as a thor-oughly credible young girl; she is too much a figure of allegory.

The Gays are part of the Old Church community in a way very different from most of the other Glasgow aristocrats. The ladies and gentlemen of *The Voice of the People, The De-liverance,* and other earlier novels had been residents and leaders in their regions for many years. The Gays, however, are relatively new in the Old Church area; for old Jonathan Gay had purchased "Jordan's Journey" when the last of the Jordans had died. Old Gay hoped to find in the country the peace he had not found elsewhere. At "Jordan's Journey" he showed the lack of consideration for others not of his class which led to his death because of his seduction and betrayal of Janet Merryweather. The Gays, though recognized as aristocrats, are despised in the community because of old Jonathan's actions and possibly because of their lack of sympathetic contact with the farm people.

Young Jonathan Gay is an anachronism in post-bellum Virginia. He fancies himself a country gentleman of leisure and expects to receive the respectful subservience of the common folk. He is puzzled when he finds that, far from subservience, he is given hatred, distrust, even scorn by the independent farm people of the region. Actually he is an object of pity. He is not a villain; he is really a rather weak, affable young man who is the slave of his own inclinations and the victim of his mother's emotional entanglements. Young Jonathan is a Southern aristocrat living in a time when he and his manner of life no longer have a place. He is unintelligent and without imagination; because of these deficiencies he loses his life.

Angela Gay presents one of several Glasgow portraits of selfish, morally weak ladies. She embodies a variety of aristocratic evil in her inability, or refusal, to admit the presence of any unpleasant fact which might violate her private comfort. Like Mrs. Blake in *The Deliverance,* Angela Gay offers an example of the working "evasive idealism"—the refusal of many Southerners to admit the presence of an evil under the mistaken notion that to admit one is to countenance it. In Angela Gay this closing of the mind is such that she does not realize her mental and spiritual blindness. All her life she has been sheltered because of her supposedly delicate heart and because of the myth of her fortitude: poor Angela has suffered so much; she must be sheltered from additional pain. Only Miss Kesiah, Angela's long-suffering sister, is aware of Angela's true nature: Kesiah knows that nothing short of physical force is likely to hurt Angela; but, then, no one pays much attention to Kesiah.

In Miss Kesiah Ellen Glasgow inquired into the life of the Southern maiden lady who did not possess beauty, money, or sufficient force of personality to break away from her world; she is doomed by custom and circumstances to a life of boredom and of possible drudgery in the homes of relatives. As a homely young girl she could not expect marriage, her only hope of escape. Yet beneath her unattractive exterior, she carries a spirit and a longing rarely imagined by those among whom she lives and who disregard her or are repulsed by her; for she wished to be an artist and even dared to hope that she might study in Paris. This, of course, was unthinkable; no lady could be permitted to go alone to Paris and much less to paint naked models. So Kesiah spent her life slaving for the lovely, "delicate" Angela, who must be guarded from every pain; but no one ever bothered whether Kesiah was ill or weary. Although Kesiah is not taken in by Angela's performance, she has lived in subjection too long to be able to do anything to prevent the evil caused by Angela's "evasive idealism."

What is the nature of *The Miller of Old Church?* Is it realistic, romantic, or tragic? It could be considered a realistic romance. It is not a tragedy, although there are tragic pathos and implications; none of the situations in this novel truly involves tragic action. Angela and young Jonathan are not tragic figures, for they lack the stature or the depth and fullness of character which the tragic character must possess. They are, furthermore, static rather than dynamic characters; they are acted upon by circumstances and by their inherited weaknesses. Such static figures cannot be tragic, however pathetic they may be.

The Miller of Old Church is a realistic analysis of social transition in post-bellum Virginia and of romantic involvements in the lives of the rural community. Ellen Glasgow was always concerned with the interesting relationships of romance and with the actualities of simple lives. As with Hardy in his novels of rural life, she never wearied of examining the intricacies in the lives of seemingly complacent, quiet communities. Even in its romantic, highly idealistic involvements, *The Miller of Old Church* reveals ironic contrasts in the lives of these people. Although given to exhibiting the ironic bitterness "under the greenwood tree" and in the fields and along the streams, Ellen Glasgow did not lose sight of the presence of romantic idealism among her Virginians. She castigated the false romance, the evils of self-pity and the "evasive idealism" while she stressed the presence of beauty and goodness in commonplace lives. The reality of the romantic and the irony of everyday existence more and more invited her feeling and wit.

Ellen Glasgow saw *The Miller of Old Church* as paralleling *The Deliverance.* She thought *The Miller* was the last of her books written in her earlier manner—a somewhat confusing notion until we realize that she is thinking that the novels which followed it reveal a different tone and style—and not necessarily different subjects.

CHAPTER 6

Portraits of Southern Ladies

IN *Virginia* (1913) and in *Life and Gabriella* (1916), Ellen Glasgow enlarged her gallery of Southern female portraits. From the beginning of her career, the novelist had studied the Southern woman as tradition, training, and circumstances had shaped her. Although Virginians of every class and stature had come under her scrutiny, she had already evinced special interest in the lady. Now she concentrated upon the forms and lives of Southern aristocratic womanhood and upon the forces which created the "ideal" lady exemplified by Virginia Pendleton of *Virginia* and the "new" lady personified by Gabriella Carr of *Life and Gabriella*.

I *Virginia*

Virginia reveals the lives not only of the Pendletons and the Treadwells in Dinwiddie but especially of Virginia, beloved child of the Reverend and Mrs. Gabriel Pendleton. Nurtured in Southern Victorian traditions, Virginia marries Oliver Treadwell, nephew of old Cyrus Treadwell, the financial master of the town. She bears three children and devotes her life to them and—so she supposes—to her husband. Oliver's youthful ambition to write good plays departs with the failure of his first serious work; he becomes cynical and gives his time to the light trash with which he achieves a despised financial success in the theater.

As years pass, he and Virginia grow away from each other. Oliver, intellectually and emotionally shallow, is caught up in his dramatic activity and occupied with an actress. Virginia's mental development had ceased at her marriage; and, before she is forty, she has become old in body, dress, manner, and mind. She cannot understand why her husband has ceased to love her, her daughters pity her, and only her son, Harry, is at all interested in what she thinks or feels. Because she is a lady who refuses to battle her opponent with sexual weapons, Virginia is doomed in her attempt to win back Oliver from his actress. Defeated, she returns to Dinwiddie and a meaningless existence in which her only hope is the prospect of her son's return.

Virginia Pendleton and her mother embody the ideal of the Southern women who in youth look toward a future in which love, marriage, and motherhood define the limits of their existence. Virginia, at twenty, lives in a bright haze of emotion; her mother exists in clouds darkened by sorrow but no less emotional. Mrs. Pendleton has been quietly happy in the affection of her husband and daughter; but, after the rector dies, she, too, soon ceases to exist physically because she had died emotionally. For Virginia, too, life had meaning only in the love of her husband. When she realizes that Oliver no longer cares for her, she dwells in a vacuum.

Mrs. Treadwell and her daughter Susan present contrasting portraits. Mrs. Treadwell had married Cyrus in haste—and spent the rest of her life regretting it. Cyrus, who can love only money, has long ago ceased to regard his wife except with contempt. He had betrayed her in her own home in his affair with the Negro servant, Mandy, who bore him a mulatto son. Mrs. Treadwell lives out meaningless days in peevish frustration; she is pitiable and despicable.

Susan Treadwell offers a contrast to Virginia Pendleton as well as to her own parents. Not so lovely as Virginia, she is physically strong, intelligent, and possessed of common sense and strength of will. Virginia, living in a mist of ill-defined idealism, is suffocated by life; Susan, able to use her mind and to feel deeply but with direction, achieves a life of meaning and substantial happiness.

Virginia is Ellen Glasgow's portrait of the Virginia lady in the days of her terrifying perfection; and the men in this novel stand in relation to this pathetic paragon. The Reverend Gabriel Pendleton complements the blind idealism of his wife; for both of these people have lived upright lives guided by a code of manners confused with a religion which dictated that one must always seek the "true view" and never admit the presence of evil. Only Gabriel Pendleton's innate manhood saves him from the vacuity of many others of his time and profession. As he had fought in the war, so he fights again in defense of a tormented young Negro and dies for what he believes right.

Cyrus Treadwell is Ellen Glasgow's acid delineation of a Southern man of money. Physically repulsive, Cyrus is even more repellent as a personality; but to the ladies and gentlemen of Dinwiddie, Cyrus is a "great man." Superbly cutting is the irony with which Ellen Glasgow shows how the ladies of the town bow before this "mammon of unrighteousness" simply because he has achieved wealth. In Cyrus Treadwell is personified the Southern idol of riches. Ladies and gentlemen, for whom everything Cyrus meant should have been hateful, bowed before his material success.

Ironic, too, is the Negro's role in *Virginia*, that of both tyrant and victim: tyrant in Aunt Docia, the Pendleton's cook; victim in Mandy and her son. Aunt Docia, once a slave in Mrs. Pendleton's family, rules the household; and, because she cannot be turned out, she tyrannizes over everyone. Mandy, the Negro servant and the victim of an evil system and its aftermath, had been used by Cyrus to satisfy his physical urges. When Mrs. Treadwell had discovered the situation, she had turned the girl out of the house—possibly the one decisive act in her life of defeat. When Mandy seeks old Cyrus's aid in saving their son from the law's exactions for killing a white policeman, his only reaction is annoyance. For the existence of his boy, he feels no responsibility whatever.

Oliver Treadwell has an effect upon Virginia: the inspiration of her youthful infatuation; the father of her children who are never more than biologically his; the husband who has ceased to be aware of her except as a part of the furniture of his life; the selfish, thoughtless but not malicious male who uses her youth, then casts her aside. Yet Oliver is no villain; he lacks the force for villainy. He is a shallow, well-meaning, but entirely selfish male. The plays with which he achieves success and which he despises as trash are really the only sort of drama of which he is capable. Perhaps Oliver's shallowness is a measure of Virginia's own lack of depth intellectually and emotionally, for to her he seems all that is excellent and desirable.

The education provided Virginia Pendleton and other girls of her generation was personified in Miss Priscilla Batte, the mistress of the Academy where Virginia, Susan, and other young ladies of Dinwiddie went through what was mistakenly thought to be education. It was

> . . . founded upon the simple theory that the less a girl knew about life, the better prepared she would be to contend with it. Knowledge of any sort (except the rudiments of reading and writing, the geography of countries she would never visit, and the dates of battles she would never mention) was kept from her as rigorously as if it contained the germs of a contagious disease. And this ignorance of anything that could possibly be useful to her was supposed in some mysterious way to add to her value as a woman and to make her a more desirable companion to a man who, either by experience or by instinct, was expected "to know his world."[1]

Virginia is a susceptible victim of this ironically ludicrous thwarting of human instincts. Susan, who asks questions even if she cannot always receive answers, escapes its worst effects. Susan even desires a college education, but old Cyrus refuses it to her partly because he cannot see any value in education for women but chiefly because he is incapable of a generous act to one of his own family.

Ellen Glasgow brought into her portrait of the lady much of her own experience. The characterization of Virginia developed from memories of the author's mother, especially with respect to her "sweetness," her enduring trouble, her self-sacrifice for her children, and even her appearance. The novelist also drew upon her own experience when she wrote of the training of the young girl. The book is an expression of Ellen Glasgow's rejection of the older definitions of the lady's role—as she had observed them—and her pitying scorn for their stultifying effects. These are represented by Virginia who, as a wife, could not share her husband's life other than to provide him physical comforts. Ironically, in an age which denied the propriety of sexual urges, she had been able to satisfy only these. Physical involvements or illness or health defined Virginia's awareness of her family's welfare. Oliver's need for sympathetic understanding when his play failed, she could not comprehend; furthermore, his need for privacy was equally incomprehensible to her. Formed in an inflexible mold, no strange ideas or liberating energies could ever penetrate her being. She had learned to believe that what she experienced was "happiness" as long as the code of beautiful behavior was never violated.

Throughout *Virginia*, failure of imagination explains the lives of the characters. Virginia's lack of imagination alienated her husband and children and left her desolate. Ironically, this same deficiency may have tempered the pain of her desolation. Susan, on the other hand, with an alert, inquiring mind, suffered disappointments courageously but also found happiness that was more than vague "sweetness." In old Cyrus, the lack of imagination created a monster; he lost the power to imagine anything unless it involved money; only his affection for Gabriel Pendleton made him human at all.

In *Virginia* Ellen Glasgow moved closer to the treatment of Southern character which later distinguished some of her best fiction. Her indictment of the culture which produced but also destroyed the old-fashioned lady may be read as a tragi-comedy of morals and manners. The characters and action arouse pity and regret before the waste of human living, concomitants of tragedy. Yet this book is not tragic, for Virginia and the others who suffer simply endure; they do not act. Virginia is pathetic; but because she neither sees nor understands, she does not attain tragic stature. Moreover, Ellen Glasgow wove into this book an Euripidean laughter through the irony which points up scene and character. The comic vision—which, like the tragic, refuses to be blinded by sentimentality or to be overcome by despair—inspires this novel.

Ellen Glasgow's conception of her material was not, however, entirely clear and her control of it not the best. The author could recognize the weaknesses which caused Virginia's troubles, but she also admired the woman into whose portrait she had introduced so much of her mother and of herself. Her affection for Virginia blurs the outlines of the story and character.

Ellen Glasgow's evocation of the atmosphere of a Southern industrial town in the last century is impressive: the presence of the tobacco factory or the railroad in conjunction with Cyrus, the ladies on their social shopping tours, the economic factors mingled in these lives without their awareness. More than in her previous novels Ellen Glasgow employed sensory images to heighten meanings. We do not soon forget Cyrus spitting on the row of dwarfed sunflowers below his porch, or Gabriel lying bleeding in the sunlit dust.

Virginia was one of Ellen Glasgow's favorite novels. Writing
to Allen Tate in 1923, she said: . . . The theme of the book is
concerned with the fate of perfection in an imperfect world.
Virginia is the incarnation of an ideal, and the irony is directed,
not at her, but at human nature which creates an ideal only to
abandon it when that ideal comes to flower. She was not a
weak character, but her vision was that of the heart. Her strength
was the strength of selfless devotion."[2]

II *Life and Gabriella*

Virginia had shown the lady as victim. *Life and Gabriella*
(1916) revealed Gabriella Carr as victor over tradition and
circumstance but as no less a lady than Virginia Pendleton.
Gabriella, rather than resign herself to genteel poverty and
dependence upon relatives, goes to work in the millinery department of Brandywine and Plummer's department store in
Richmond, although her doing this irreparably shocks Mrs. Carr
and the other members of the family. She also breaks her
engagement to "dear Arthur" Peyton, the perfect—and ineffectual
—gentleman, and waits eagerly for George Fowler, handsome
and New York-bred, to come to claim her heart. Gabriella's
marriage to the lazy, selfish, disloyal Fowler goes to pieces
before her husband's drunkenness, his inability to earn a living
or provide a real home, and his betrayal with another woman.
Gabriella gives all her devotion to Fanny and Archibald, her
children, and to Mr. and Mrs. Fowler, George's parents.

Mr. Fowler fails in business and dies; George goes off with
Florrie Spencer, once Gabriella's friend in Richmond. Gabriella
then makes a home for herself and her children—with the assistance of Miss Polly Hatch, a little seamstress from Richmond—
and goes to work in the dressmaking establishment of Madame
Dinard. By the end of ten years she controls the business.
Eventually Gabriella meets Ben O'Hara, who has risen from
street-urchin poverty to railroad-builder wealth. She is both
attracted and repelled by him. When George Fowler comes to
her to die, O'Hara takes charge during the brief illness and the
funeral.

After an eighteen years' absence, Gabriella returns to Richmond for a visit. She finds that Arthur Peyton has amounted to
little in the law, for he clings to old ideas and ways. She sees

him now plainly, for he is shorn of the romantic veil in which her imagination had enveloped him. When she returns to New York, she pursues Ben O'Hara to the station before he can return to the West and leave her forever. She gets to the train in time!—but has she really escaped her illusions?

Life and Gabriella, an interesting novel as well as a very uneven one, mingles the characteristics of comedy of manners, success story, domestic romance, and social history. Ellen Glasgow never seems to have determined clearly just what she wanted to show in it—other than that a Southern girl, Gabriella, might create a worth-while life for herself, achieve some happiness, and still remain a lady; or that the Southern lady need not be a victim of circumstance and the code of gentility. The image of Gabriella is blurred because Ellen Glasgow again introduced into her character too much of herself and was unable to develop the character in the novel with sufficient perspective. At times, Gabriella may have become the woman which the novelist liked to believe herself to be.

Because the book refutes *Virginia*, it appears contrived; too much is "arranged" in relation to the pattern traced in the earlier novel. For example, Gabriella's mother, Mrs. Carr, is a fainter, more repressed, less Southern lady than Mrs. Pendleton of *Virginia*. George Fowler resembles Oliver Treadwell in that he is selfish, fascinates the heroine, and ultimately betrays her; he differs from Oliver in being less a human being and more a motivating element in the plot. Oliver had personality; George has only appearance.

Although Ellen Glasgow did not decide whether she was presenting Gabriella as a vindication of the Southern lady or the "new" woman, she, living at the turn of the century, may be viewed as an example of the emancipated female whose gradual winning of freedom had fascinated Henry James and William Dean Howells. Gabriella often appears as the "new" woman in business, going to battle in the business arena undaunted by any difficulty or embarrassment. Ellen Glasgow's Gabriella offers a difference, of course: she is a *Southern* lady venturing into the New York business competition. One of the novelist's purposes seemingly was to show that Gabriella could not only survive but conquer without losing her feminine graces, her concern for her children, or her sexual attraction.

Understandably, Ellen Glasgow did not venture very far into

the mysteries of business—even into the dressmaking and millinery business of Mme. Dinard.[3] As in earlier books, New York functions more as a land of make-believe for Ellen Glasgow than as an actual city. Problems exist in abundance for Gabriella, Miss Polly, and the Fowlers. Yet the New York portion of the novel always carries an air of the exotic and the possibility of some sinister adventure. It rarely possesses the conviction of actuality conveyed by the New York scenes of James or Edith Wharton, or by Ellen Glasgow's Richmond scenes.

If Gabriella is the "new" woman, then Ben O'Hara is a version of the self-made man who has risen from the city poverty to wealth and power in a vaguely defined West. Telling of Gabriella's friendship and love for O'Hara gave Ellen Glasgow an opportunity to explore the idea of the common man in America more explicitly and extensively than she had considered his story in the South in her earlier novels.[4] Although O'Hara had his prototype in an Irish businessman whom the author had known during her residence in New York, he is a figure of romance rather than a revealed person. Both Gabriella Starr and Ben O'Hara in this "success" story act in an Horatio Alger narrative of the rise from rags to riches.

Life and Gabriella in the opening chapters carries the tone and the emphases of social comedy which Ellen Glasgow had occasionally exhibited in her earlier writing and which she later developed with greater skill. In the chapters set in Richmond and in Gabriella's visit to her home near the end of the novel, the comic vision is evident in the lighter, satirical interpretation and in the keener penetration into personalities and circumstance. After Gabriella marries and goes to New York to live, the texture of the prose becomes heavier; the rhythm of the action is slowed; the tone henceforth is nearer that of domestic romance than of social comedy. Despite the lugubrious note, however, the over-all effect is comic.

We could wish for more scenes in the novel such as Jane Carr's rushing home to her mother, the family conclave which followed her leaving Charley near the beginning of the novel, Gabriella's going to work in a store in Richmond to the consternation of her mother and the rest of her relatives, or her return to Richmond near the end of the book, with the sketch of the reformed Charley who is now the model of a Virginian Babbitt years before Sinclair Lewis created the epitome of the booster.

And of course "dear Arthur" Peyton and Gabriella's Dream of Love are the very stuff of comedy.

It is also interesting to note that Ellen Glasgow used the phrases "the sheltered life" and "vein of iron" frequently in this book. "Vein of iron" appears at least seven times. "The sheltered life," mentioned in passing, carries the ironic implications which Ellen Glasgow would explore brilliantly in the novel for which that phrase served as a title some sixteen years later: the evils and dangers in lives devoted to maintaining appearances and the evasion of ugly realities. The "vein of iron" in this novel refers to the strengthening character elements which preserved Gabriella and to their absence which resulted in the demoralization of George Fowler; the mischief of Florrie Spencer; and the desiccated, shadowy failure of Arthur Peyton. For Ellen Glasgow, "vein of iron" has not in this book acquired the special significance of a religiously induced force of personality which it has in *Barren Ground* and even more specifically in the novel which she called *Vein of Iron*.

Ellen Glasgow continued in *Life and Gabriella* to exhibit certain inequities of style which she never quite removed from her work. Some of her American gentlemen use "jolly" in their conversation in a manner which destroys an illusion of reality in their speech; even Ben O'Hara, New York Irishman, does so! And a character goes to a "chemist's" rather than a drugstore in one scene. These Briticisms suggest Ellen Glasgow's never quite surmounted feeling that she must nod to England. On the other hand, her prose in this book is usually clear, fluent, and effective. If her writing in it lacks the brilliance of some parts of *Virginia* or of most of the writing in her later social comedies, her ability is more than adequate for revealing her immediate perceptions.

III *Inferior Publications*

The Builders (1919) and *One Man in His Time* (1922) are inferior to Ellen Glasgow's better fiction and, like the earlier *The Wheel of Life* and *The Ancient Law*, do not merit extended discussion. *The Builders*, as has been shown, is pertinent to Ellen Glasgow's political interests. Written during the time of the novelist's love affair with Henry Anderson, it evidently reflects his, as well as the author's, political point of view. But a political treatise is not good fiction. Too much of *The Builders* reads as though the characters were addressing a public meeting. And much of the remainder of the novel anticipates such domestic melodrama as that in Daphne du Maurier's *Rebecca*. But some good things are in the book: the characterization of Angelica Blackburn, for example, rewards those who relish portraits of completely selfish, wholly evil women who may be pitiable in their evil. Too often, however, the novel slides off into neo-Gothic sensation when it does not present thinly veiled political disquisitions.

One Man in His Time was written in the period when Ellen Glasgow was recovering from her tormented love affair with Henry Anderson. Apparently, she was unable in this period of turmoil to use effectively all the forces of her mind and imagination in the composition of this novel. The book reveals the materials of a political novel, a social comedy or tragi-comedy, and a romantic melodrama. Cut from the same cloth as *The Builders*, it is better integrated than the earlier book; but its tone is as uneven as the novel which had preceded it. Awkwardly handled melodrama follows passages and chapters of social comedy. Somehow the story of the radical Virginia governor and his daughter hardly rises above the tone of sensation fiction, and it never clearly belongs to the story of aristocratic Corinna Page and her friends. Although Ellen Glasgow wrote in this novel of political and social change in the South, she was not at this time imaginatively captured by her material.

The Shadowy Third and Other Stories (1923) brought together in one volume seven short stories which Ellen Glasgow had written in the past two dozen years. None of these stories is poor, but none is a masterpiece of short fiction. Although the novelist recognized early in her career that she worked best in the longer form of the novel, she essayed short stories occasionally for periodical publication. Three of the stories in this collection show her interest in the supernatural and especially in the possibilities of ghostly manifestations for fiction. The others pose moral riddles. This book and Ellen Glasgow's fugitive short fiction show clearly that she was not at ease within the limitations which the short story imposed upon character development and thematic involvement. For the effective working of her imagination, she required the wider areas of time, space, and character portrayal which the novel provided.

CHAPTER 7

The Rewards of Fortitude:
Barren Ground

TO *Barren Ground* (1925) Ellen Glasgow brought most of what she had learned in a rich but tormented existence. She believed that, in her fortitude and her ironic view of humanity, she possessed the means of defending herself against the on-slaughts of circumstance. Out of her own sorrow, anger, resent-ment, despair, rationalization, and hope for something better, she created the pattern of Dorinda Oakley's life. Out of her love of beauty and her faith in the fortitude which she believed sustained her, Ellen Glasgow drew the sources of Dorinda's survival, if not her triumph.

In *Barren Ground* Dorinda Oakley appears first as a girl of twenty who is alive with the bloom of her newly-awakened love for Jason Greylock. In the final pages, she is a woman of fifty who has lived through betrayal, hard work, and a long renunciation; she believes that she has triumphed over the hostile forces around her, and even over the threat to her peace of mind and the loss of her soul. She thinks, as did her creator, that she has learned to live without happiness but to live a good life.

Between the girl of twenty and the woman of fifty, Dorinda has loved and been loved by young Jason Greylock—and then betrayed by him when pressure was put upon him to marry Geneva Ellgood. Dorinda has seen the years of her New York interlude when she had sought refuge among strangers, lost her child by Jason, and worked for two years. She has witnessed her father's death and his defeat by the land which he had used unwisely; and she has observed her mother's destruction because of her love for her worthless younger son Rufus and because of the torment of her puritan conscience after she had lied to protect him from the exactions of justice.

Dorinda has also seen the years of hard work at "Old Farm" while she transformed the place from the run-down, poorly cultivated acres to a thriving dairy farm. She has seen Jason Greylock descend into his private inferno of drink, decay, and disease, while "Five Oaks" went to pieces and had to be sold—to Dorinda—for taxes and while his wife, Geneva, went mad and drowned herself. Dorinda has also known a marriage of convenience but respect to Nathan Pedlar, the storekeeper, and she has received Nathan's body after his heroic death when trying to save the people in a wrecked train. At last she has seen the death of Jason Greylock, worn out with drink, consumption, and loss of spirit. As she surveys her life, she believes that she has conquered through fortitude and hard work all the forces that might have destroyed her. She assures herself that she has known a worthy life.

I *The Levels of Society*

For *Barren Ground* time and place are inextricably woven into the lives of Dorinda and her neighbors. The country of *Barren Ground* is the border area in Virginia where the Piedmont uplands shade into the low Tidewater, a gently rolling, almost level region which, in the time of the novel, is given to broomsedge, pine, and scrub growth but which once had produced tobacco and corn. Little tobacco would be found in this part of Virginia now, and the modifications described in the novel are now reflected in the dairy farming and timber cutting of this part of the state.

The neighborhood of Pedlar's Mill suffered from the plague of tradition and of refusal to try something new and from isolation and poor transportation. Although the railroad between Richmond and Washington passed through the village, the outlying farms were cut off during the winter by impassable roads and poorly bridged streams. This isolation pervades the novel and the lives of its people.

Ellen Glasgow thought of the story as stretching from 1894 to 1924, from a period when the results of the Civil War were still felt in the South—although the new political and social burgeonings were evident—to the unsettled years just after

World War I. And the people of *Barren Ground* illustrate the social and economic shadings of this period in the Virginia community, for Ellen Glasgow took considerable pains to make clear the variations of caste. Dorinda Oakley and her family represent the class of poorer white people in the post-bellum South; they are not "poor white trash," but they are linked by marriage and propinquity to that depressed group. The Oakleys are independent farmers who own their land; but their "Old Farm" really belongs to Mrs. Oakley, who had inherited it from her father and grandfather, stalwart Scotch Calvinists, who had come into this region from farther west in Virginia. Mrs. Oakley represents, therefore, a class somewhat higher in education and general cultural attainments than that of her husband who is of that "border" class of white farm people who may rise to some affluence and respectability or who may sink into penury and the "trash" classification. The Oakleys are poor white farmers, but they are landowners, not tenants or sharecroppers.

Perhaps a rung or two higher on the social and economic ladder are Nathan Pedlar, storekeeper and miller (there had always been a Pedlar as miller at Pedlar's Mill); Mr. Kettledrum, the veterinarian; and Miss Snead, who does dressmaking in the neighborhood. Those most nearly the aristocrats of the region are the Ellgoods and the Greylocks. The Ellgoods are progressive in matters of farming, but they are also the only persons who have the money to improve their land.

The Greylocks, father and son, are decadent aristocrats who exhibit the weaknesses of their class. Once a good physician, old Dr. Greylock has become a victim of drink, inertia, and his own meanness and moral collapse. His son Jason, who lacks the moral stamina to resist his father and the other pressures put upon him, surrenders to isolation, drink, and a feeling that he is doomed. The scenes at "Five Oaks," involving the old doctor and his brood of mulatto children begotten on the yellow girl who lives with him, may compare with the work of William Faulkner or Erskine Caldwell for depiction of human degradation and surrender to sensual satisfactions for their own sake. But this phase of the life of these people is not overdone as it is in some Southern writing which substitutes corncobs and inertia for moonlight and magnolias.

The Negroes of *Barren Ground* constitute an important element in the community. Most of these people have lived in it for many generations, first as slaves, then as tenants, or more often as small landholders on farms purchased from their former masters or other white neighbors. Respectable, hardworking people, many of them, untrammeled by the agricultural traditions of their white neighbors, have become good farmers. They are, of course, still uneducated and gripped by most of the superstitions of their heritage. Many of these Negroes form the labor force for "Old Farm" when Dorinda develops her dairy farm; but Ellen Glasgow shows that they must be supervised for, unless Dorinda watches them carefully, only rarely can they be depended upon to do things as she wishes them done.

Two of the Negroes stand out in the book: Aunt Mehitable, the old ex-slave, and Fluvanna, the younger woman who becomes Dorinda's valued assistant and trusted friend. In these two, Ellen Glasgow embodied in strong-willed, superstitious, and shrewd Aunt Mehitable the excellences of the old-time Negro, and in Fluvanna the capable, energetic, and faithful "new" Negro of the turn of the century.

These colored folk are not amusing "humor" figures or sinister creatures of melodrama. They are a simpler, more ignorant people, viewed in the light of fact and not as elements of sociological theory. Ellen Glasgow's portraits are of men and women, not of idealized figures. Since "Old Farm," Pedlar's Mill, and the neighborhood had their prototypes in Louisa County where Ellen Glasgow had spent happy summers as a small girl, many of the Negroes and some of the white characters grew out of people she had known in those far-off days.

Although some critics were misled by the facts of the story and, unable to see beyond them, assumed that the central idea of *Barren Ground* was the recovery of worn-out land in the South, the account of Dorinda's rebuilding of the land and the farms is always subordinate to the spiritual meanings. The land and her work on it are significant to Dorinda, but the important element is the drama of her developing personality—the struggle and the triumph or defeat of her soul.

As a book intimately concerned with the people of a part of the South and with the meanings of their lives in relation to its larger life, this novel is properly a regional study. It differs, however, from the usual "local color" writing because the author is not satisfied with a mere surface treatment—a gentle consideration of the quaint customs of her back-country farm folk—for

Ellen Glasgow not only resented having her fiction labeled as Southern or Virginian but thought of it as universal in meaning. Certainly, *Barren Ground* and the novels which follow it have this universal applicability.

II *Character Is Fate*

The central theme of *Barren Ground* is as old as Greek epic and drama, older perhaps than recorded literature: Character is Fate. Although Ellen Glasgow did not discard her evolutionary faith nor her interest in heredity and environment, she showed throughout the novel that she believed that human lives are, ultimately, "determined" by the factors which comprise the character of each individual.

Joshua Oakley, Dorinda's father, could never be other than a defeated, ineffectual, poor farmer. He lacks too many requisites for success: daring, imagination, knowledge, initiative, and freedom not only from a paralyzing tradition but from his sense of inevitable defeat. He loves the farm; he could live nowhere else; but the land swallowed him long before he lay buried beneath it.

Dorinda's mother represents most of the weaknesses and strengths of her Scottish, Calvinist people. Mrs. Oakley is another of Ellen Glasgow's women who are sustained yet tormented by religion. In her flows the "vein of iron" of her Scottish Presbyterian faith. From it she draws the strength which enables her to endure poverty, illness, and a life holding no hope of material improvement; but, when she lies to protect another, the violation of her soul crushes her as if she had been struck by a powerful hand. She had once loved a missionary to Africa; and, when he died, she had experienced near-madness when she saw visions of faraway lands. She had fallen in love with young Joshua Oakley when he had had the appearance of a young John the Baptist. Although Mrs. Oakley seemed to have little in common with her feckless husband, theirs had been a successful marriage. Mrs. Oakley had lived a hard life with little apparent reward; still, we cannot say that her days were wasted.

Nathan Pedlar, the storekeeper and later the husband of Dorinda, is a man ahead of his time; he knows much that his neighbors do not, but his knowledge seems inconsequential to them. Nathan, ironically, in his death creates a legend of heroic action which promises to supplant the memory of the actual man. Because we see Nathan almost entirely through Dorinda's eyes, our view of him may be somewhat confused; for Dorinda never quite knew how she felt about Nathan.

Jason Greylock is one whose life is determined by his weakness. He is despised by his drunken father, who has forced him to study medicine and then compelled him to return to Pedlar's Mill. He is a well-meaning, amiable man who lacks the stamina to do what he knows is right or to withstand evil either in himself or others. He is not a villain, for he has not the strength of mind and soul for villainy. When Dorinda would hate him after he betrays her, she realizes the difficulty of hating so empty a thing as Jason. Yet she can never shut him out of her life.

For Dorinda, character is fate. She refuses to be defeated by betrayal in love, by poverty, or by hard work. The "vein of iron" in her heritage, which, in her mother, had brought only profitless labor and a willingness to endure, provides in Dorinda the strengthening element which enables her to withstand disappointment and even despair. The willingness to work, which her father possessed, is in Dorinda transmuted into purposive activity. Her revolt against the life she sees around her becomes a rebellion against the crippling effects of traditional agricultural methods.

Dorinda learns to draw from within herself and from her surroundings the strength she needs. If for a long time she rejects the God of Wrath of her mother's Presbyterian faith, she does not reject the God of Beauty. Hers is the hardness of one who has found a source of strength in her belief in herself, and she has escaped the sapping effects of frustrated bitterness. Work out of doors has strengthened her body and not harmed her beauty, which had always been of a solid, handsome variety rather than of a delicate prettiness.

Yet Dorinda Oakley has not entirely escaped the consequences of her decisions. She has found fortitude a reward in itself. But she still remembers that she had missed the ultimate rewards of love, and she cannot deny the reality of the loss. Her independence has brought with it a spiritual loneliness as well as an arrogance which sets her apart even from those whom she most cherishes: her stepson, John Abner; her husband, Nathan.

Dorinda has sustained a wound which makes her triumph less than complete. Apparently her ecstatic experience of love with

Jason and her revulsion after his betrayal have caused her to carry with her an abhorrence of physical love. She marries Nathan with the understanding that the marriage shall not be physically consummated, and Nathan is willing to accept this. Although the marriage may be a measure of Nathan as well as of Dorinda, neither she nor apparently Ellen Glasgow seems to have considered the extent of Dorinda's selfishness. Into this phase of Dorinda's portrayal, Ellen Glasgow introduced much of her own attitude toward love and marriage, just as she drew upon her own emotional experience in her development of Dorinda's story.

III *The Novel's Superiority*

Barren Ground is superior in design and construction to Ellen Glasgow's earlier novels. By centering her narrative upon Dorinda, she maintained a tightness of structure and an inevitable movement of action interrupted in only one important respect. The interlude in New York when Dorinda conveniently suffers a miscarriage is out of harmony with the rest of the novel, for New York serves as a means for getting around a structural difficulty. Less obtrusive defects are those portions of the narrative in which characters are removed who might interfere with concentration upon Dorinda. Of this sort are the deaths of Mr. and Mrs. Oakley; the hurrying of Rufus to the city and out of the story; and even the demise of Nathan, although this event has justification in the irony inherent in Nathan and his life. Although she took pride in her powers of imagination, invention was not Ellen Glasgow's strength as a novelist; and this lack is evident even in one of her finest novels.

Especially noteworthy in *Barren Ground* is Ellen Glasgow's use of symbolic imagery. The three parts of the book are subsumed under the symbols of broomsedge, pine, and life-everlasting: broomsedge has associations with betrayal of the land and of Dorinda and with an enveloping, smothering tradition; pine, its connotations of strength, beauty, and a sustaining belief in growth and hope of achievement; and life-everlasting, its meanings of beauty in a world of material achievement and of life achieved in spite of hardship and disappointment.

All through the early portions of the novel run images of

flowing, rushing, running, moving water; these are integrated with the development of Dorinda in her eager youth, her aspiring to growth and achievement, and her desire for a life of love and delight. These water images also suggest the possibility of growth and fertility in the midst of sterility and defeat. Water may also provide an ironic suggestion when it is associated with the revelation of Dorinda's pregnancy, which is followed almost immediately by the breaking of the storm and then by the horror of Dorinda's encounter with old Dr. Greylock who reveals Jason's betrayal when she takes refuge from the storm at "Five Oaks."

Images of cold and hardness also highlight the meanings of the narrative. They are associated with the blighting effect of the untimely frost which can destroy Joshua Oakley's tobacco crop when he has left it out too long. But these images of cold and inflexible things are also associated with changes in Dorinda's character.

A form of symbolic imagery is Ellen Glasgow's treatment of time in this novel. Not only does she indicate the natural passage of months and years, but she also interprets the erosion of time upon the lives of her people. Throughout the book "time" is a force touching some individuals lightly, ripening others, and scarifying a few as though the very passage of moments were an eroding substance carving out character and personality. We see this effect especially in Mrs. Oakley, whom time has destroyed, and in Dorinda, whom time has changed and shaped but who has withstood its destruction. For Dorinda has clearly not entirely escaped time's touch: she has grown deeper in character and strength of personality but not without the loss of much that the reader can observe and of which Dorinda herself is aware. Although Dorinda has learned to survive through fortitude and to find value in her life, she has missed the love which she values supremely; and in this realization lies in part her tragedy. One rather obvious circumstance may be observed: the story of Dorinda's life begins in late spring, with the promise of warmth and growth soon to come; the story ends in autumn after the death of Jason, with Dorinda looking forward to her last years.

Ellen Glasgow developed for this novel a style which is neither gloomily depressing nor disconcerting as a too lively or epigrammatic diction would be. The narrative, interspersed with its dramatic scenes, moves with dignity and has apparent inevitability. Although there is much that is somber, the grey light is frequently brightened by the color that is always present. We may come away from *Barren Ground* with the impression of darkness lit up with ever-recurring light and color—a symbol of the nature of human life which the novelist endeavored to suggest. Although Ellen Glasgow's use of language continued to follow traditional lines, she experimented with a tentative stream-of-consciousness effect useful in bringing out meanings where the usual narrative or dialogue forms would not serve. She later carried this experimentation in style much farther in the novels after *Barren Ground*.

Barren Ground possesses both epic and tragic qualities. It has the heroic movement and character development associated with epic literature; scenes, people, and actions are somehow larger than in ordinary life. Yet Ellen Glasgow did not carry this epic suggestiveness beyond the limits of the realities in the lives of her people. She escaped the somewhat blurred, even distorted effect often noticeable in the writings of Elizabeth Madox Roberts, such as *The Time of Man*, where the activities of ordinary folk take on an almost supernatural quality.

Dorinda Oakley is, in some respects, a tragic figure although her story as presented in *Barren Ground* is not actually a tragedy. Despite all her achievement, Dorinda's life represents a loss, a waste of love. Although she has achieved material success and although she tells herself that she has made a good life, she is less than whole because she has excluded passion from her existence. Such a view does not presuppose that all lives which have missed love are blighted, but for Dorinda this loss involved tragic waste. In her had been the potentiality for love which might have made her life more valuable for herself and others. Her experience with Jason had destroyed that possibility, or so she had come to believe; she knew herself the poorer for this loss.

Neither Dorinda nor her creator were clear about the final assessment of Dorinda's life; and apparently Dorinda reflects much of Ellen Glasgow's uncertainty. Had Dorinda triumphed through hard work and fortitude? Ellen Glasgow would like to believe that she and her character had achieved such victory. Yet the closing pages of the novel suggest that Ellen Glasgow partly realized that, though Dorinda had escaped destruction, she had not entirely conquered. She had been involved in a tragic loss; this she could not escape. Dorinda, looking back over her years, seems to try to convince herself that she has won her victory over hostile forces, but she is not certain. What she thinks to herself does not ring with complete conviction; and, because Ellen Glasgow may have been trying to convince herself of her own victory, the significance of Dorinda's life is blurred. The novelist needed to believe that she had learned to live without love, that fortitude and the power of beauty were enough; yet she was not sure.

Several times in *Barren Ground* Ellen Glasgow observed that the pathos of life is worse than the tragedy. Throughout the novel we realize the pathos of these lives; indeed, the involvement in pathos all through the book is painfully pervasive. We experience sympathy and pity in contemplating the lives and deaths of Mr. and Mrs. Oakley, of Jason, or even of Nathan; we become aware of the irony of their existences; but these are not figures of tragedy.

But *Barren Ground*, as Dorinda's story, suggests Greek tragedy. Doubtless, Ellen Glasgow gained much from the suggestion of parallels to the love, betrayal, and subsequent hatred of Medea and Jason in Euripides' play. *Oedipus at Colonnus* also comes to mind in the portrayal of Dorinda at the close of the story; for she, like the aged Oedipus, had gained serenity of soul. The Virginia girl and the old Greek thought that they had found a resolution in a haven where, all passion spent, they could rest from emotional and physical struggle.

Barren Ground suggests, therefore, the essentials of ancient tragic meanings: the waste of valuable life in Dorinda's loss of love and in her denial of emotion; the *hubris*, or the pride and the susceptibility to emotion and later her ardent belief in her own destiny; and the stature of character, for Dorinda becomes a magnificent woman. All these factors suggest a tragic work, but one element is lacking: awareness. The reader cannot be certain that either Dorinda or Ellen Glasgow was fully aware of a tragic meaning; for, as has been noted, their final vision is blurred in the almost sentimental ending which mars, without seriously injuring, a distinguished work of art.

In her essay in *A Certain Measure* about *Barren Ground* Ellen Glasgow wrote of its origins as deeply rooted in her own experience in Virginia, the meaning of Dorinda to her, and the relation of the novel to her other studies of Virginia in transition and especially to *The Sheltered Life*. She gave much attention to the social status of the people and to the significance of the land in Southern culture.[1] She wrote elsewhere in *A Certain Measure* that

> . . . it was not until I began to write *Barren Ground* that I was able to orient myself anew and to respond to a fresh, and, apparently, a different, creative impulse. All that came after this period was the result of this heightened consciousness and this altered perspective. Unimportant as it may appear in a final summing up of actual endeavour, my later way of writing began suddenly, after a long apprenticeship to life, in a single intuitive visitation. But the struggle to this end had been difficult; . . .[2]

CHAPTER 8

A Rage of Manners

THREE NOVELS published after *Barren Ground* represent Ellen Glasgow's commitment to an ironic view in her interpretation of Southern manners and morals. *The Romantic Comedians* (1926), *They Stooped to Folly* (1929), and *The Sheltered Life* (1932) are concerned with related aspects of the code of polite action. Southern, and even more specifically Virginian, these novels extend far beyond geographical and chronological boundaries to encompass timeless, limitless meanings.

In her novels of manners Ellen Glasgow essayed a literary form which has not enjoyed popularity in America. Cooper ventured into the novel of manners, but this aspect of his writing is not typical of the author of the Leatherstocking Tales. Howells wrote novels of American society; it may be debated whether their material or tone is that of the novel of manners. Henry James and his disciple, Edith Wharton, were two of the most effective interpreters of men and women in their social-moral significances.

Ellen Glasgow had been concerned from the beginning of her career with the central problems of the novel of manners: the nuances of social class distinctions in the South; their continued meaning or their loss of it in the post-bellum years; the changing status of members of the lower classes in relation to an also changing, often decaying, aristocracy; the strengths and weaknesses inherent in the Southern code of polite behavior and their effects upon its adherents or victims; and the meaning of social tradition in the lives of Southerners. In all of her novels the close relation of manners and morals is evident, but it is especially observable in *The Romance of a Plain Man, The Miller of Old Church, Virginia,* and *Life and Gabriella.*

Neither tragedy nor comedy thrives in a climate lacking agreement in matters of belief or action—in one in which a moral code has ceased to exercise a controlling force. Western society during the past century has been affected by such a loss of belief and by the lack of a binding moral code. Various forms of unbelief or pseudo-faith have taken the place of religions. Material ends have replaced spiritual goals. For many twentieth-century Americans, a pragmatic code of action has taken the place of a traditional code of manners and morals: Is it profitable? Is it pleasant?

In the novels which compose her triptych of manners, Ellen Glasgow explored the meaning for her Virginians of a change in moral attitudes. In these novels she showed plainly that she could neither accept nor wholly reject the code of behavior which had governed polite society or, indeed, all of society in Virginia since colonial times. Earlier she had attacked the features of that code which she found debilitating, or even evil in their effect. Especially had she objected to what she called "evasive idealism." For against all forces in the life of an aristocratic society which prevented men and women from living rich lives, or which protected barbarity, weakness and greed in the name of tradition, Ellen Glasgow sternly waged war. Yet, if she attacked the code as faulty, she could not readily accept what was usually offered as its alternative: the abandonment of all rule in human relationships.

I *The Romantic Comedians*

The theme of *The Romantic Comedians* is as old as man and woman: the marriage of an elderly man to a young wife. Judge Gamaliel Bland Honeywell moves from the formal observations of his loss of Cordelia, his wife of more than thirty years, to courtship of and marriage to Annabel Upchurch, a lovely girl of twenty-three summers and the daughter of Mrs. Bella Upchurch, an impecunious widow of impeccable lineage. Judge Honeywell's marriage fails because of the disparity in ages; Annabel's delight in parties, dances, and normal youthful activity; and his desire to maintain his home and his existence in the manner to which he had become accustomed.

Though the Judge blesses his young wife and his mother-in-law with luxuries for which they had longed, he cannot provide

Annabel with the youthful husband she finds and takes when young Dabney Birdsong comes along. She and Dabney go off together, and Judge Honeywell reaps only a chill and a subsequent illness from his efforts to persuade her to change her mind. But as the Judge recovers from his illness, he looks at his nurse and feels the stirring of spring once again in his blood.

This simple, even obvious narrative is the central structure upon which Ellen Glasgow organized her novel. Out of the relationships of the Judge, Annabel, her mother, his sister Mrs. Edmonia Bredalbane, and his departed wife Cordelia, the novelist wove a fabric of scintillating light and color, or, to vary the metaphor, a pattern musical in its development of variations on this comedy of passions. Indeed, the procedure through which we delight in the activities of men and women in love, or out of love, is essentially that of an interweaving of observations about the comedy of their activities.

Queenborough—Ellen Glasgow's creation of the essence of all Virginia towns—is the setting for *The Romantic Comedians*. Although there are touches of other Virginia towns and cities in Queenborough, Richmond furnished the primary ingredients: old streets, old homes with cherished furnishings and precious memories, and a small society not only of "old" families secure in their knowledge of generations of gentility but of traditions slowly succumbing to the incursions of industry and of the traditionless. The physical actuality of Queenborough is vaguely sketched in several homes, a few streets, and the cemetery where Judge Honeywell brings flowers to Cordelia's grave. Only this suggestion is needed, for Queenborough really functions as a state of mind, an atmosphere, a creation of time and space that is the sum of all the lives, beliefs, assumptions, and mistaken notions which have existed along these streets and in these rooms.

The Romantic Comedians is that jewel in fiction: the serious interpretation of life which is a joy for the reader. Our delight in the play of Ellen Glasgow's wit or in her malicious yet never ill-tempered thrusts at the foibles of her ladies and gentlemen may prevent us from perceiving the artistry of the book and the keen wisdom of its pages. Throughout this novel, Ellen Glasgow subjects human struggles to the clarifying, cleansing effects of the silver laughter of comedy; and the focus of the comic vision eliminates the confused and blurred views of sentimentality or "evasive idealism." Always, as in serious comedy, our laughter is very close to the tears of tragedy; we see people and their actions as participants in the follies of the comic genre; but we see, too, that a very slight shift of emphasis may reveal a tragic mask upon the actors. In *The Sheltered Life* the manner and the tone are frequently comic, but the ultimate emphasis is tragic. In *The Romantic Comedians* and in *They Stooped to Folly* the emphasis is comic, but there are tragic overtones.

Among the characters of *The Romantic Comedians* is Miss Amanda Lightfoot, the belle of yesterday, who had quarreled with Gamaliel Honeywell and who had then spent the rest of her life being faithful to her early love. Gamaliel had met the late Cordelia on the boat when, as he thought, he was pursuing Amanda. Widower Judge Honeywell respects and admires Amanda but shrinks from marrying her; his eyes are turned toward more youthful, slimmer figures than Amanda's well-proportioned form. And poor Miss Amanda continues to play her lady's role as she had learned it in her youth.

Edmonia Bredalbane—the Judge's twin sister and a fallen woman who refused to admit her ruin and instead marched forth to four husbands, a grotesque figure, and a vigorous age—is the source of some of the more delightful passages in the novel. Of her reputation Edmonia remarks:

". . . As provincial as you are in America, it is hopeless to try to make you understand that behaviour as much as beauty is a question of geography, and that my respectability increases with every mile of the distance I travel from Queenborough. In France, my reputation is above reproach; by the time I reach Vienna, I have become a bit of a prude; and contrasted with the Balkan temperament, I am little more than a tombstone to female virtue."[1]

Of the nature of happiness Edmonia may echo her creator when she remarks to her brother:

". . . I've always believed that happiness, any kind of happiness that does not make someone else miserable, is meritorious. That, my dear brother, is what you held against me in Queenborough. You Episcopalians may have made most of the history and all the mint juleps in Virginia; but you have left your politics and your laws to the Methodists and Baptists, and pleasure-baiting has always been the favourite sport of those earnest Christians."[2]

Cordelia, Judge Honeywell's late wife, is ever-present in the pages of the novel though absent from the actual scenes. Although Judge Honeywell cannot recall just how Cordelia looked, he cannot relinquish her effect: the habits of his life with her are a part of him; the furnishings of his home and the diet which she had so carefully supervised are forever present. Ellen Glasgow successfully and delightfully contrived to make the departed Cordelia one of the actors in her drama. From scarcely a page is she absent, for neither the Judge nor his young Annabel can remove themselves from her influence. She exercises her force through no supernatural power, of course; she continues to exist for the Judge quite simply because she had long ago become a part of his thought and feeling without his realizing it.

These characters of *The Romantic Comedians* might have become representations of human foibles or sheer monsters if the hatred of the author had functioned rather than a certain degree of malice. Ellen Glasgow did not hate these people; they are not monsters, nor are they the flat figures of stage comedy. They move from the pages of their story as rounded, thoroughly alive individuals who possess their own personalities and gain individuality through their relationship to the other actors in their drama. They are people, not puppets.

The humanity as well as the humor in these portraits of manners is nowhere more evident than in Ellen Glasgow's portrayal of Judge Honeywell. She laughs at him, of course; but even when this laughter is most tinctured with malice, it is tempered with tenderness and pity for the folly of such elderly gentlemen—indeed, of all weak-willed, susceptible males. She does not despise him nor forget his humanity. And of the search for happiness and love Ellen Glasgow through her creation Mrs. Upchurch, who frequently represents the author's attitude, observes that she

. . . had considered the disadvantages, in man or woman, of an incurably amorous habit of mind . . . that even the insidious irony of the modern point of view had scarcely damaged the popular superstition that love and happiness are interchangeable terms. Old and young and perennially middle-aged, she beheld the world enslaved by this immemorial illusion. Was she herself, she sometimes asked, the only person who had been able to maintain a true sense of values and an equilibrium of the emotions? Judge

Honeywell with his law and learning; Amanda with her exalted character and her simple wit; Annabel with her artless sophistication; . . . all this company of happiness-hunters appeared to be little better than a troupe of romantic comedians.[3]

The structure of *The Romantic Comedians* suggests a circular motion in its arrangement of time and space as well as in the thoughts and emotions of the characters, and especially in those of Judge Honeywell: from springtime to springtime, away from Queenborough and back to Queenborough, from the Judge's youthful burgeonings to disillusion and back to illusion once more. This circular motion is analogous to the recurrent folly of mankind, but it is not simply the particular folly of an elderly gentleman's attempt to recover his youth in the arms of a young wife. Around this central element Ellen Glasgow wove a pattern of irony which etches the paradox of the whole book: the contrasts of man's romantic aspirations to the actualities of his existence, and the awareness that the realities of man's existence may actually be shaped more in terms of these ideals than according to the apparent actualities.

II *They Stooped to Folly*

They Stooped to Folly (1929) is subtitled "A Comedy of Morals." Ostensibly its central theme is the idea of the "ruined woman," of what her "ruin" consisted, and of the ironic contrasts involved in changing attitudes toward her. The morals of this comedy, however, extend beyond the relatively simple problem of the violation of a sexual code. Essentially, this book is about a topic that is so often the subject of platitude that it might seem hopelessly outworn: what men and women live by is not simply what they *think* they live by; it is something which exists in the inner depths of their being and motivates all their actions. Ultimately, the subject of all high comedy may be what ladies and gentlemen create as pretenses to support their behavior, their belief in those pretenses, and the ironic contrast of these notions to their actual motives.

They Stooped to Folly tells of three "ruined women" of three generations from the vantage point of the 1920's. One of them is poor Aunt Agatha Littlepage who had slipped once in her youth and had lived ever after a life of seclusion in the third-floor, back bedroom of her nephew's home; only World War I and a time of relaxing attitudes had brought a slight measure of liberty to poor Aunt Agatha: she had been encouraged to sew for the soldiers (pajamas), and she had become so free as to develop a taste for sentimental moving pictures and for banana splits. A "ruined woman" of a later generation is Mrs. Dalrymple, who had been the center of a scandal that had shaken Queenborough. After a divorce and a period of service in war-torn Europe, Mrs. Dalrymple—lovely, lovable, and willing as ever to be loved—had returned to Queenborough. In another age and place she might have been a cherished courtesan; with the more limited opportunities of Queenborough she is both delightful and, in her way, dangerous. Milly Burden is the youngest of the ruined ladies. Where poor Aunt Agatha and Mrs. Dalrymple had not denied that they had violated the code of sexual behavior, Milly simply refuses to recognize the existence of the code or the fact of her "ruin." She had given herself to Martin Welding because she loved him. When he went away to Europe, she still loved him and wanted him back.

The story of *They Stooped to Folly* concerns the lives of these women in relation to Mr. and Mrs. Virginius Littlepage; their daughter, Mary Victoria; and Milly's wandering lover, Martin Welding. Mr. Littlepage—a Virginia gentleman, a prosperous lawyer in Queenborough, and Milly's employer—arranges to have Mary Victoria, who is in war-torn Europe "rescuing" people, look for Martin. Mary Victoria finds him, marries him, and brings him back to Queenborough to the consternation of the Littlepages and the freeing of Milly Burden from her emotional bonds. For Milly no longer harbors her illusions concerning Martin and herself.

They Stooped to Folly offers revelation and interpretation rather than simply narration. The division of the book into three parts entitled "Mr. Littlepage," "Mrs. Littlepage," and "False Spring" suggests the structure and point of view. The first part presents Mr. Littlepage's vision of his life and present situation; the second that of his wife, Victoria; and the third weaves together the strands of these lives.

In addition to the central figures, others have their roles in this comedy of morals: Mrs. Burden, Milly's mother, is another of Ellen Glasgow's presentations of the distortions of spirit created by the puritan conscience. Mrs. Burden is guided by the idea that she has certain "rights" and "duties" toward others and that she should expect comparable ones in return. Her monstrous notion of "duty" has driven her husband from her and is driving Milly away; Mrs. Burden is conscience gone sour.

Martin Welding has the artist's temperament without his temper. He is the man whom women think they love and whom men often despise: he is a weakling physically and spiritually, yet attractive in his dark charm. He becomes the victim of Mary Victoria Littlepage's mania for reform and of Milly Burden's independent, somewhat arrogant spirit and passion. His role as the "seducer" of Milly and as the seduced husband of Mary Victoria is ironic and delightfully horrible. Ultimately, Martin escapes once more from women (he wants only isolation from feminine possessiveness) when he leaves Mary Victoria, who turns her attentions to their unborn child.

Mary Victoria Littlepage is a beautiful, blonde Boadicea with an incurable notion that she is destined to modify everything to conform to her idea of what it should be. She is convinced that she has a perfect right to interfere in other lives simply because *she* believes that she should do so; and whatever she thinks or feels, is, of course, inevitably right. When she meets Martin Welding in Europe, she promptly assumes that the other women in his life have been "the wrong sort" for him and that she, of course, is the right type. She is another side of that coin of conscience rampant; the other is symbolized by Mrs. Burden. Where Mrs. Burden glooms her life away over her "rights" and the "duty" of others to her, Mary Victoria throws out her chest and marches forth to *assert* her rights and duty—and tramples everything beneath her. Occasionally, Mr. Littlepage is aware of her overwhelming arrogance, but he is helpless in his adoration of his daughter.

The Littlepage sons, Duncan and Curle, suggest views of life common in the 1920's. Duncan sees life sardonically, darkly; he is willing to stand aside and watch the circus of his age. Curle is the twentieth-century booster—another of Ellen Glasgow's brief sketches of the businessman whom Sinclair Lewis made memorable. Had she not already drawn a preliminary sketch for Curle Littlepage in *Life and Gabriella*, we might suspect that Babbitt had posed for his portrait; for, like Lewis' Babbitt, Curle is superficial, brash, boosting, and a believer in something he thinks is progress. His father finds it difficult to stomach this son.

Louisa Goodard is the eternal clubwoman. She is devoted to the Littlepages, but especially to her friend Victoria. Louisa, a brisk, very active spinster, is a busy mover in many good works without being either a fanatical reformer or a troublesome busybody. In her lively efficiency and good sense she is at times exhilarating. She has been loved for many years by Virginius Littlepage's brother Marmaduke; and during this same time, as Marmaduke well knows but Virginius does not, Louisa has hopelessly loved Virginius, her dear friend's husband.

Marmaduke Littlepage, "modern" painter of outrageous nudes in primary colors, is one of Ellen Glasgow's truly civilized men. He is not taken in by the evasions and the shams which substitute for reality among his contemporaries; he is, as he points out to Virginius, genuine; and he refuses to pretend to be something he is not. Marmaduke is no hero or saint; he is a very real human being who is subject to his own weaknesses and difficulties. The loss of a leg during the war has shifted the course of his life; it perhaps made him more spectator than actor.

The fact that Marmaduke is crippled may raise a question with regard to Ellen Glasgow's civilized people. An earlier "civilized man" Uncle Tucker in *The Deliverance* was crippled by the loss of a leg; he, too, was potentially a painter. General Archbald of *The Sheltered Life*, John Fincastle of *Vein of Iron*, and Asa Timberlake of *In This Our Life* are all "cripples" but not physically. Each of these men has been "hurt" by circumstance and has sustained a psychic or spiritual wound which has permanently changed him. Each has become, like Marmaduke Littlepage, "genuine"—one who refuses to pretend to himself any longer. And each has become more an observer than a participant. Interestingly, all of Ellen Glasgow's most civilized people are men. Did she mean that only the male mind and spirit possess the capacity for being civilized? Or did she suggest that only the man withdrawn from the rush of life, the observer of both virtue and folly, can achieve the balanced vision of the civilized human being?

Victoria Littlepage is that most difficult of all characters to delineate in fiction: a good woman who is neither stupid nor dull. In the pages of *They Stooped to Folly*, the reader shares with Mrs. Littlepage the closing months of her life. Outwardly she has lived as a typical woman of her class for whom the freedoms and restrictions of the code of beautiful behavior and the liberal tenets of the Episcopal Church have seemed sufficient. She had tried to ameliorate the sternness of poor Aunt Agatha's imprisonment, and she had stood by Virginius when he moved against the current of genteel convention in befriending Amy Dalrymple and serving as her attorney. She had even tolerated her husband's admitting Milly Burden into his office. Her love for Mary Victoria blinds her, however, to her daughter's character. Moved always by what is for her the highest idealistic motives, such an excellent woman might easily be dull; but Victoria Littlepage is actually very interesting. Perhaps this interest derives from the fact that, as Marmaduke observes, she is not only an idealist but she, too, is genuine. Whether she is also a civilized person, according to Ellen Glasgow's standards, the reader may judge.

Victoria Littlepage, in some measure, shares the more objective point of view of Ellen Glasgow's civilized gentlemen because she, too, has been "wounded." She has achieved a spiritual vantage in these last months of her life, for she has learned that she can live only a short time. She does not seek death; neither does she fear it. She has found life interesting and often pleasant. She keeps the knowledge of her approaching death from Virginius and her children and goes about her daily activities. Yet this mortal knowledge gives her a new angle of vision. Without in any way assuming for herself superior understanding, she finds that the storms of daily existence do not seem so important. As she grows weaker, she often turns away from the strife of others' living and longs only for peace from the soundless tumult that she feels roaring about her. Ellen Glasgow does not sentimentalize over Victoria nor assume that she is dying in a heroic manner. She simply presents a once beautiful, still attractive, apparently conventional lady achieving, as she nears death, a changed vision of herself and of her life.

The theme of the "ruined woman" unifies *They Stooped to Folly*; but Mr. Virginius Littlepage, rather than any of the "ruined" women, provides the central point of view and Ellen Glasgow's means of examining the nature of modern morals. His role is to represent the failure of the Southern code of gentility. Quietly, subtly, through Mr. Littlepage, Ellen Glasgow demonstrated how that code of behavior could encourage sham, deceit and cowardice; how it could substitute appearances for ideals and actualities. Even more subtly, she demonstrated through Virginius that his weaknesses as a Southern gentleman were shared by men and women of his aristocratic assumptions in regions beyond Queenborough and across the Mason and Dixon line.

The kinship of Ellen Glasgow's Virginius to T. S. Eliot's J. Alfred Prufrock has been noted,[4] for both exemplify the man who has suffered a loss of moral nerve. Outwardly, Virginius is a distinguished lawyer who is also the heir of the traditions of family, class, and profession proper to a Southern gentleman. He, like Prufrock, has learned how to assume the appropriate masks for the usual circumstances of his life; but the reader can pierce through these for a look into Mr. Littlepage's soul. This counterpoint of the ironies of his outer and inner lives is brilliantly developed, and the satirical mockery of his portrait is no less devastating for being drawn in warm grays rather than etched with acid.

Virginius Littlepage's complacency shields a conventional and timid spirit. He represents, too, a willingness to substitute softness and sentimentality for true sensibility. Though he has liked to think of himself as a free soul—one who has dared to go against the current—he realizes, when now and then he "awakens," that actually he has remained within the restraining bonds of his notion of what a gentleman should be. In this "code" he has found neither the strongest support nor a source of joy in life: his notions of the actions of a gentleman have permitted him to lust after Mrs. Dalrymple and even momentarily to contemplate a passing "affair" with her without, of course, conceiving of his actions as in any way involving a betrayal of his wife or resembling the betrayal of Milly Burden by Martin Welding, his son-in-law. (One was the "fancy" of a gentleman, of course; the other the dastardly act of a cad.) All in all, Virginius Littlepage is a charming, respected citizen of Queenborough who lacks the courage of his inclinations, whose somewhat pompous appearance substitutes for dignity, whose good fortune it has been to attain position in spite of mediocrity. Where Ellen Glasgow laughed with light mockery at Judge Honeywell in *The Romantic Comedians,* her comic tone in *They Stooped to Folly* carried a harsher quality.

They Stooped to Folly Ellen Glasgow analyzed in *A Certain Measure* as her treatment of a man-imposed woman myth—that of the "ruined" woman. She thought of the book as a notable essay in the comedy of manners as well as a novel of city life in her history of manners in Virginia. She found particular satisfaction in her creation of Victoria Littlepage, the lady who should have been a dull, subordinate figure but who insisted upon becoming clear and interesting.[5]

III *The Sheltered Life*

The Sheltered Life (1932) is Ellen Glasgow's finest novel, for in this tragedy of manners she combined most effectively all the elements of her material and art. In it character, action, and atmosphere interact to reveal not only the tragedy in lives shaped by the code of polite behavior and by the pretenses of a cult of Beauty but also the evil lurking in assumptions of innocence. She cast over these people a magic portrayal, a brilliance of life, and a beauty which makes superb the irony in the charm of their outward lives and their darker implications.

On Washington Street, in a once fashionable but now decaying neighborhood of Queenborough, live General David Archbald; his daughters, Isabella and Etta; his daughter-in-law, the widow of his beloved son; and his granddaughter, Jenny Blair. Not far away live George and Eva Birdsong. In the pages of *The Sheltered Life* all move as they are revealed through the eyes and hearts of the old man and the young girl, Jenny Blair. One sees them when the old general is seventy-five and Jenny Blair is almost ten, then later when he is eighty-three and eighty-four and Jenny Blair seventeen.

Jenny Blair's childish admiration for George Birdsong becomes a passionate infatuation as she nears womanhood. She believes that she adores the ailing Eva, but she thinks that she can love George and receive his attentions without hurting anyone. Eva becomes ill, endures a hysterectomy and a long convalescence, and, the shadow of her former beauty still faintly visible, returns to Queenborough. One evening just after George has returned from duck hunting, Eva discovers Jenny Blair in his arms. She calls her husband into the next room; in a moment a sound of gunfire shatters the peace of the afternoon. George lies dead; the gun at her feet, Eva sits before him with a frozen smile on her face. And Jenny Blair can only throw herself into her grandfather's arms with a cry, " 'Oh, Grandfather, I didn't mean anything! . . . I didn't mean anything in the world!' "[5]

Queenborough, the urban setting for the action of *The Sheltered Life*, is—as in *The Romantic Comedians* and *They Stooped to Folly*—Ellen Glasgow's imagined Virginia city into which she breathed the atmosphere of the older Virginia towns she had known: their old streets and houses, their fading yet still persevering customs, and their changing culture. The Queenborough of *The Sheltered Life*, however, is drawn much more from the novelist's own Richmond than any town of the previous novels. Washington Street, with the homes of the Archbalds and the Birdsongs, is taken almost directly from the neighborhood of Main and Foushee streets where Ellen Glasgow lived, and some touches of her home enter into the description. More important, however, than the physical resemblance is the representation of the neighborhood as a decaying district of industrial dirt and evil odors from which most of the older residents have moved to more fashionable areas.

Ellen Glasgow used skillfully the device of two points of view in *The Sheltered Life*. As we have noted, everything is filtered through the mind and emotions of General Archbald and his granddaughter: through the experience of the old man to whom life has given no shelter and of the child and then of the young girl whom custom and her family supposedly shelter within innocence and ignorance. Ellen Glasgow's ironic vision clothed these lives with universal and tragic meaning.

Mrs. Archbald, the General's widowed daughter-in-law, is a Southern lady who has found a substitute for thought in the precepts of manners. She was not unintelligent; she simply substituted for disturbing thought a much more satisfactory, charming manner and cast of countenance with the appropriate emotion to accompany them. In contrast to her, Isabella Archbald, whose concerns move on the periphery of the central action, emphasizes the suffering inherent in the lives of the other characters while showing the possibility of a lady's rebelling against custom if she dares. High-spirited, attractive, passionate and unwilling to surrender to the pressures of the aristocratic code, Isabella refused to permit a timid youth and a thoughtless violation of the usual proprieties to blight her life. Instead of weeping or piously retiring to an upper room after inadvertently acquiring the appearance of improper conduct, Isabella looked upon Joseph Crocker, carpenter and plain man, saw that he was good, and married him.

Of course her sister-in-law, Mrs. Archbald, found it simple to convince herself, with the aid of a genealogist, that Joseph's family was descended from the "real" Crockers, that his people were "quiet" rather than "plain"—even if they were Baptists rather than Episcopalians: ". . . When so few standards remained unimpaired, the distinction between plain people and quiet people was almost obliterated by the first important step from the Baptist Communion to the Episcopal Church. And everything, of course, was made easier because Joseph had so little religion. . . ."[6]

Jenny Blair's poor Aunt Etta, the General's other daughter, was not immured like some Southern spinsters because of an error. Instead she, as a physiological mistake, was doomed to misery. Not only plain, but definitely lacking in any charm to attract masculine eyes, Etta suffered illnesses induced by inhibitions and frustrations, turned her natural desires into scarcely suppressed Lesbian passions which alienated woman friends, and fretted away her days reading yellow-backed French novels or having her nose packed at a young doctor's office. Now and then Etta appears in a bitterly ironic aspect. She, who is without beauty and can never be loved but only pitied, adores Eva Birdsong for her loveliness—and Eva's beauty has brought her only heartache.

Eva Birdsong embodies a myth and is its victim: she is the personification of the Southern Beauty; she is crushed by the demands of that myth. With deft irony, Ellen Glasgow presented Eva in all her cruel glory before illness and the strain of living up to the demands of the cult of Beauty had crushed her. Near the end of her career of pretense Eva tells Jenny Blair: " '. . . When you've never been yourself for forty years, you've forgotten what you are really. . . . I'm worn out with being somebody else—with being somebody's ideal. I want to turn round and be myself for a little while before it is too late, before it is all over.' "[7]

George Birdsong, Eva's charming but ineffectual husband, had found it too great a strain to be worthy of so idealized a being as his wife. He sought his satisfactions in more mundane interests such as hunting and drinking; having casual encounters with younger, less charming, but easily approachable girls such as Delia Barron; or enjoying the warm flesh of his mulatto mistress, Memoria. George is neither mean nor evil; he is simply weak and careless; but he is generous to a fault. For example, the General can never forget that, when George had inherited a small fortune, he had offered it to him to help him over a moment of economic embarrassment; a little later George had just as readily frittered it away in bad investments.

George adores his wife after his fashion, but his fashion does not include fidelity of body or mind. Although he would never deliberately hurt her, he is naïve in supposing that his infidelities can be kept a secret from Eva. He can deny himself a drink or a cigarette while Eva is in the shadow of death, but he cannot see that she requires a more vital loyalty. Because he has never really been aware of himself, he cannot give himself to Eva. He, too, is the victim of the Southern code of "beautiful behavior" which accepted the notion that a man might "know his world" and play any number of roles in it but still be admitted as a member in good standing in a society in which his wife had to move in a more restricted area.

Memoria, George's Negro mistress, is sympathetically portrayed as both a force and a victim. When an infant, she had been rescued from a burning house by "gallant" young George Birdsong. As a woman, she serves as the Birdsong's washerwoman and as the instrument of her rescuer's physical satisfaction. She is neither heroine nor villain; she's a capable, handsome woman who is respected and even admired by the white community of Queenborough which really never condemns her though it suspects her role in the drama of the Birdsongs.

Memoria shares in the initiation of Jenny Blair into the adult world of Queenborough when the little girl falls on the walk in front of her house and the colored woman picks her up and carries her into her home. There Jenny Blair discovers George Birdsong; without realizing the meaning of his presence in Memoria's house, she agrees to share with him the delightful thrill of a "secret": they will not say anything about her accident nor about George's being in Memoria's house. So at the age of nine years and seven months Jenny Blair becomes a part of the duplicity and passion sheltered behind the screen which her class cherishes as propriety.

Jenny Blair Archbald, the lively, imaginative child, grows to the brink of womanhood in a carefully protected environment in which her elders follow the policy of their class in attempting to shield her from all awareness of evil or unpleasantness.

Actually, Jenny Blair understands much more than her mother and grandfather admit: but admitting it, she would be no longer innocent—and, of course, the pretense of innocence had to be preserved! From a natural, often charming little girl, she becomes a pretty, selfish young woman whose circumstances have conspired to teach her that to be loved is really the ultimate goal for the women of her class, whatever may be otherwise pretended.

For Jenny Blair and those dearest to her, the innocence and self-centered existence of childhood become in her ripening young womanhood the sources of mortal danger. Spoiled by her family and sheltered by custom, Jenny Blair seeks only her own desires. She has learned nothing to prevent her believing that, so long as she does not *intend* to harm anyone else, she may satisfy her own pleasures. Her mind so conditioned, she can think that she adores Eva Birdsong and at the same time desire George's more than avuncular attentions. Hers is the tragic evil inherent in a sheltered innocence.

John Welch, Eva Birdsong's cousin, who has grown to manhood in the Birdsong home, symbolizes a new generation which rejects the shams of the older and assumes a more realistic attitude. He and Jenny Blair do not like each other; for he sees through her shallow, superficial self, and she cannot endure his awareness. To the Birdsongs and the Archbalds he seems a very nice young man who is too much in earnest about reforming the evils he sees around him. He tolerates George and adores Eva; but he recognizes, at least in part, that her unhappiness is the result of the strain of lifelong sham and frustration.

General David Archbald has lived a long life without ever doing anything which he really wished to do. Born into a society which ritualized cruelty and inhumanity, the child David could not conform; he had been regarded, therefore, as a "mollycoddle" by his sportsman grandfather. After he had assisted a slave to escape, he had been shipped abroad until people forgot. He had enjoyed the love of women but had lost the girl who might have brought him happiness; for, trapped by a snowstorm and the rules of propriety into marrying a girl whom he did not love and who did not love him, he had endured a lifetime of marriage, begotten children, fought dutifully in the Civil War, and won recognition in his profession. Yet none of this had he desired. Even in his later years as a widower, when he had wished to marry again, he had been restrained by the knowledge that he could not hurt the women of his family who depended upon him.

David Archbald had wished to be a poet in a time and place which never tolerated poetry except in calf-bound volumes bearing the names of foreign authors. He is also a humanitarian in a society which cultivated cruelty and insensitivity as a fine art and provided cock-fighting for the lower orders and fox-hunting for ladies and gentlemen. A sheltering and sheltered gentleman, he lives in a society in which woman pretends to obey but actually gently and inexorably dominates. As General Archbald in old age reflects upon his life, he is wise, yet not all wise; sadly weary, yet not embittered. In the most consuming affections of his old age—his love for Jenny Blair and for Eva Birdsong—General Archbald has not been able to escape the illusions of his class: he could not dispel the myths of Jenny Blair's youthful innocence nor of Eva's imperishable beauty. Yet David Archbald is that rarest creature, whether gentleman or commoner, the civilized man. Although Ellen Glasgow created a number of such men, General Archbald may offer her most perfect embodiment of this concept.

In *The Sheltered Life* Ellen Glasgow employed time as an extra dimension. She had earlier experimented with such a projection of the meaning of time, notably in *They Stooped to Folly* in those passages concerning the insights of Virginius Littlepage. In the section of *The Sheltered Life* which she called "The Deep Past," she enveloped her characters in a sheath of time. The reader moves back and forth through time; for he is in the immediate present of the evening before Eva Birdsong's operation and of the evening of David Archbald's life, but at the same moment he shares with the General all his life's experience. The reader also recognizes that time has been an eroding force in the false life of Eva Birdsong; the years have worn away her beauty and at last her will to live.

The Sheltered Life is a tragedy of manners, and we witness the tragedy of attrition in which suffering and the loss of time—of much living of great value—results from conformity to custom. General Archbald saw his soul scarified in a life of doing what was required rather than what he believed and desired. Eva Birdsong was worn away by a life-long performance of a role in which she had been cast by nature and by the society into which she had been born. Both persons endured suffering and lost what was of greatest value to them: General Archbald at great cost preserved his soul and himself; Eva sacrificed herself —and her soul—on an altar dedicated to Love and Beauty. Both characters possess the dimensions of tragic character: stature as persons, the capacity for feeling, awareness, and the potentiality for greatness—but all these are thwarted by circumstances.

Through *The Sheltered Life* moves a tragic rhythm in the pattern of tensions and conflicts; there is also an ever-increasing though slightly noticeable awareness of suffering and endurance until one reaches the last catastrophic scene in which all forces are concentrated not only in the moment of violence but in the realization of what all these lives mean to General Archbald, to Eva, and to the reader. This rhythmic curve of *The Sheltered Life* rises from the first quiet movements of the opening passages in "The Age of Make-Believe," through the gradually increasing intensity of "The Deep Past," to the final action of "The Illusion." We may realize the emotional force of this movement in the suffering, frustration, and loss which comes to its culminating stroke as Eva Birdsong sits with her husband's gun at her feet, George is dead in the chair before her, and Jenny Blair can only weep that she didn't mean anything.

The Sheltered Life is Ellen Glasgow's finest work of art. Into it she poured all the resources of her understanding of life and also the skillful craftsmanship born of her long endeavor in her art. In the style of the book she exhibited a sense of taste and an understanding of the demands of her subject and material which were close to perfection. Tone, timing, and deftness of touch are also combined to convey precisely the mood—and the meaning in it—requisite for each passage of narrative, dialogue, and commentary. Symbolic elements, such as the pervading neighborhood smell, function in an usually ironic counterpoint against the lives of the Archbalds and the Birdsongs. Throughout the novel, in the language, in what the language states, and in what is left unsaid, the current of irony carries with it clarity of idea and feeling, illuminates scene and character, and underlines the tragic meaning.

The ideal of classic art was "nothing too much." In composition and style *The Sheltered Life* exemplifies that ideal. Ellen Glasgow thought that the novel should illuminate life; the tragic light provided in *The Sheltered Life* is such an illumination.

CHAPTER *9*

Modern Man and the Search for Meanings

VEIN OF IRON (1935) and *In This Our Life* (1941) are not a sequence, nor do they form parts of a trilogy or tetralogy with *Barren Ground* and *The Sheltered Life*. Both *Vein of Iron* and *In This Our Life* are, however, closely related not only to each other but to these earlier novels in material, tone, themes, and characters. All four emphasize growth and decay in a changing social order; a transition in social and moral values or an actual loss of values; and the role of manners in an increasingly unmannered, amoral barbarism calling itself civilization. In these novels, as in her other fiction, Ellen Glasgow explored an ultimate question: what can be the role of fortitude for men and women who live, as Thoreau believed, "lives of quiet desperation."

I *Vein of Iron*

In *Vein of Iron* Ellen Glasgow tells of the Fincastles who live in Ironside, a small village hidden in the mountains of the upper valley of the James River, a part of the Great Valley of Virginia; and she presents her chronicle largely from the point of view of Ada Fincastle and partly through the eyes of Ada's father, John, and of Grandmother Fincastle. The Fincastles live in the manse which Ada's Presbyterian forefathers had built and had occupied since first they came to the Valley. John Fincastle had followed in their steps part of the way, for he had the prospect of becoming a leading minister until his unorthodox beliefs resulted in ejection from the ministry. He ekes out a living teaching "profane" subjects to the village children, working in his garden, and laboring on his five-volume philosophical work.

John Fincastle had married Mary Evelyn, a delicately nurtured girl from eastern Virginia; and Ada, their daughter, is a child of ten years at the beginning of the century when the narrative opens. Mary Evelyn in her frail beauty had seemed destined to move in pleasant paths, but in her life with John she had seen deprivation and the poverty of life in Ironside. She lives with a smile which becomes almost a grimace of nervous exhaustion, and she dies worn out but without regret.

John Fincastle's indomitable mother is the mighty rock who sustains the family and binds it fast to her and to the manse in Ironside. Even though John's heresy is a terrible shock to the woman who has lived by the stern tenets of the Presbyterian faith, she has stood by her son. She is a power of physical and spiritual strength not only in her family but also in the mountain community. Her influence pervades the whole book and especially the earlier portions of the story.

John Fincastle's unmarried sister, Meggie, completes the Fincastle household. She is one of Ellen Glasgow's happy, richly endowed spinsters who are pleasant contrasts to other portraits of embittered old maids. Aunt Meggie, probably patterned after the author's own Aunt Rebecca, is typically Scottish in her ways: she is industrious and religious, but her religion is tempered with moderation and good sense.

Ada Fincastle provides the center of interest in events which move from the turn of the century, when she is ten years old, to the middle 1930's when she is a mature woman. In Ada are suggestions of other Glasgow women—especially of Dorinda Oakley. Although her inheritance religiously and socially is comparable to that of Dorinda, she is a very different person in her reaction to the buffets of life. Though, like Dorinda, she is scarred by hardship and disappointment, she never becomes hardened. In her, as in the other Fincastles, runs the "vein of iron" of endurance and resistance to evil and difficulty. But her "vein of iron" is a tempered, almost steel-like quality, which has endowed her with resilience and spiritual force. She and the other members of her family are not victims of "evasive idealism"; furthermore, they do not take refuge in the shams and pretenses of polite manners. They are, however, in their sterner fashion cultured people.

Closely associated with the Fincastles are the Rowans, the wealthiest people in the village; Dr. Updike, the physician, who might have married Aunt Meggie; Mr. Black, the minister; and Mrs. McBride and her son, Ralph. Mr. Rowan is the local merchant and small industrialist of the community. He and his wife have spoiled their only daughter, Janet, a child who looks like the young Queen Victoria but lacks that monarch's morals.

Mrs. McBride is a Calvinist gone sour; her religion brings her and her son misery. She has preserved her sense of evil without understanding the evil in her own attitude and in her treatment of her son Ralph whose life she has made miserable and whose outlook she has twisted before he is grown; only his Irish charm inherited from his father has partly saved him. Mrs. McBride is a worshiper of a God of Wrath; she has never dreamed of a God of Love. Though she does not realize that her greatest delight is hate, she was never so happy as during World War I when she had an ample target for her bitterness. All that she feels and does is, she believes, in accord with her religion. She is duty degraded and religion distorted.

Ralph McBride has loved and been loved by Ada since they were children. He is a handsome, capable, lively boy and youth whose good mind and abilities indicate the possibility of a career in the law. He studies with John Fincastle and anticipates marrying Ada. He reckons, however, without the turns of fate, his own weakness, and the machinations of a mean-spirited girl.

In several remarkable chapters Ellen Glasgow takes the reader into the lives of the Fincastles to show what they felt and thought as they sat about the manse fire. We see Ada through her bitter disappointment when she cannot have the doll with real hair because there is not enough money. When Ada is grown, she must endure an even greater disappointment in her loss of Ralph. Ralph lacks resistance to the pressures of society; he cannot take a dare, and he can be persuaded to drink even though he knows he cannot handle whiskey. Then he lets himself be trapped by Janet Rowan into being found in her bedroom after a dance.

Although Ralph insists that they had done nothing wrong, the rules of propriety say that Janet has been compromised and that Ralph must marry her. So even in the mountain village the shams of polite society combine with the stern rules of a religiously guided community to force the boy, already engaged to Ada, to enter into a marriage of hate with Janet. Ada's father and grandmother support Janet's father and the minister, Mr. Black, in compelling Ralph to marry the girl in the belief that what they are doing is "right"; what the girl claims must be believed in such cases.

Janet and Ralph waste six years in quarreling and, on Janet's part, in unfaithfulness. World War I comes, Janet is about to get a divorce so that she can marry someone else, and Ralph returns from army training to Ironside. He and Ada go off to a mountain cabin for a few days of love before he leaves for the war. When Ada realizes that she is pregnant, she refuses to tell Ralph because she knows that he will worry and that he might do something rash. Ada's pregnancy, of course, very nearly breaks the heart of Grandmother Fincastle. She insists that Ada should write to Ralph; that he should be made to suffer; and, of course, that both Ada and Ralph have sinned. John Fincastle is more tolerant; he insists that Ada is good. Knowing the temper of this puritan community, Ada remains at the manse. When the child is born, Grandmother Fincastle relents toward Ada and supports her in her need.

Not long after the birth of Ranny, Ada's and Ralph's son, Grandmother weakens and dies. The Fincastles move to Queenborough, where John finds a place as a teacher in a girls' school and Ada works in a department store. When Ralph returns from war, he goes to work as an automobile salesman; all thought of studying law is forgotten. During the 1920's he prospers, but the joy of life has departed from Ralph, who lacks Ada's vein of steel; yet he and Ada are reasonably happy together. John Fincastle finishes the last volume of his philosophical work, but it receives little notice from anyone except a handful of philosophers scattered about the world.

Though Ralph loves Ada, he allows his attentions to wander to Minna Bergen, the empty-headed daughter of their neighbors. When he and Minna are out in a car one night, there is a smashup and Ralph is seriously injured; a long convalescence follows before he recovers from the resulting partial paralysis. When the Depression comes to Queenborough, Ralph, Ada and John lose their jobs. Some of their neighbors face starvation or charity. John Fincastle, old, wornout, and knowing death is near, makes his way back to Ironside so that he can die at the manse. As the novel ends, Ada, Ralph, Ranny, and Aunt Meggie will return to the manse and presumably to a better life than they have known in Queenborough.

Queenborough is, in *Vein of Iron,* Richmond, even to the name of an actual area such as Jackson Ward for the Negro district. In this Richmond of the post-World War I and the Depression years, the old traditions and customs still prevail for the older generations, but the fiber of moral strength has weakened. In those years Queenborough, like the rest of America, bowed before money. Ellen Glasgow skillfully dramatizes the contrasts of the new, shallower views with those of John Fincastle.

Through *Vein of Iron* Ellen Glasgow moves the shuttle of time as she creates her fabric of human history. The Fincastles, like most of the inhabitants of Shut-in Valley, have lived in this mountain-valley region of Virginia since frontier times. All through the book, Ellen Glasgow enriched her story of the Fincastles with accounts of their earlier, sterner days when Indians had carried off Great-great-grandmother Tod. From other stories current in her family, Ellen Glasgow drew the memories of Hunter's and Sheridan's Civil War depredations, and the essence of the early experience of the Fincastles. Mrs. McBride possesses the religious attitude of the author's father in her bitter worship of a God of Wrath rather than one of Love. And Mary Evelyn is endowed with the loveliness, charm, and sensitivity of the novelist's mother. Grandmother Fincastle seems an invention of the novelist's imagination—a creation shaped out of all the finer, if sterner, and richer, if harsher, qualities of those Scotch-Irish Calvinists whose "vein of iron" had been tempered in the furnace of experience. These people have grown strong in their strict if tempered piety; but, although they are solid people of rich human quality, they would not be regarded as aristocratic by Mary Evelyn's gentle family of the Tidewater. Furthermore, not all of these Scotch-Irish possessed the same "vein of iron"—the quality of fortitude and the belief in excellence —which belonged to the Fincastles. Some like the Rowans are materialistic; although successful in accumulating the world's goods, they are poor in spirit. Mrs. McBride's conscience is twisted.

Ellen Glasgow's own heritage entered into the making of *Vein of Iron.* The phrase which serves as a title had long been with her as an image of endurance in the face of disaster and of qualities of personality and character which inhered in some human stock and which might sustain fortunate individuals. Moreover, Ellen Glasgow came to believe that this "vein of iron" belonged especially to the Scotch-Irish Calvinist settlers of Virginia from whom her father came. The complex of qualities it symbolized might be present in other human strains, but these hardy Christians seemed to exhibit it most often. Others of her characters had revealed their "veins of iron," but the Fincastles and their associates provided its most dramatic exhibition.

John Fincastle, another of her civilized men, was endowed by Ellen Glasgow with her own attitude toward religion and philosophy. She tried to create in him the philosopher and believer in a God different from the one of Calvin; yet John Fincastle exists, however, independent of his creator, as a personality with his own life in his own world. But Ellen Glasgow also attempted to create in John Fincastle a philosopher-saint. Perhaps such a being can only be *suggested* in a novel; in any case, the reader finds only suggestions of these dimensions in John Fincastle. Ellen Glasgow could not demonstrate her character's philosophical stature; she could only imply his greatness. His spiritual purity and his attainment of something near the exaltation of the Eastern mystics are more effectively dramatized than his philosophical distinction.

John Fincastle is a civilized man; all the Fincastles are civilized in another but perhaps more popular sense. They had brought with them into the Valley standards of living, a hard yet rich religion, a way of life which they had preserved and through which they had, in a degree, civilized their frontier community. Where other settlers had been conquered by circumstances and had relinquished what vestiges of European culture they had possessed to become little more than savages, the Fincastles had built churches, cleared farms, taught their children both sacred and profane learning, and brought their own culture into the forest. The leaders among the Scotch-Irish settlers had been their preachers; these preachers had been scholars, even philosophers after their fashion, though rarely so unorthodox as John Fincastle. A philosopher in Shut-in Valley offered, therefore, no contradiction of probabilities.

Ralph McBride possessed the same heritage as Ada, but the puritan conscience of his mother has distorted his childhood. He lacks the "vein of iron"; in its place he harbors only darkness and a resentment against his mother and the circumstances which, he feels, have robbed him of a right. Weaker than Ada or John Fincastle, Ralph is neither evil nor mean; he is still essentially good, but he lacks the temperament and the inward light which enable Ada to endure disappointment and to find life worth while without pretending that it is not difficult. In a larger sense, Ralph McBride represents the men of his generation—as Ellen Glasgow understood them: he is well-meaning, charming, bright or even brilliant, moderately ambitious yet easily turned aside by difficulties. Lacking spiritual sustenance and confidence in himself or in his star, he is easily tempted, fundamentally decent, and capable of crumbling easily in bad times.

Some readers have believed that Ellen Glasgow condemned commerce and urban culture and preached in this novel an agrarian policy. John Fincastle and his ancestors had not been farmers but preachers, scholars, and leaders of the people. The manse at Ironside has a small amount of land around it, not a farm; and, when Ada and Ralph plan to return to it, they do so for reasons which have little to do with a return to the land, as such. Ralph intends to sell automobiles and perhaps farm implements; they will have the manse and its garden for shelter and food and the hills, valleys and mountains and clean air around them. Theirs is a return to their spiritual home, which should not be interpreted as the novelist's doctrinaire rejection of industry for agriculture.

Vein of Iron is less perfect in design than *The Sheltered Life,* for the division of setting between Ironside and Queenborough may seem to create two related stories rather than one complete novel. This division, however, provides a useful contrast in customs and attitudes: that of the withdrawn, isolated community of the Valley to that of the commercial atmosphere and old Tidewater society and traditions of the eastern Virginia city.

The style of *Vein of Iron* is excellently suited to its purposes; but it does not exhibit the brilliantly epigrammatic qualities, the irony of wit and commentary, of the three previous novels of manners. Instead, the style is fitted to the people of the book and the movement of their lives; it is rich in evocative imagery, and it moves with steady, solid yet never heavy rhythms suggestive of the strength, force, and tempered steel of the Fincastle character. The style of *Vein of Iron* is successful also in its power to suggest clearly the characters as wholly rounded individuals, each vivid in his own idiosyncrasies yet never a caricature; these men and women are alive. Setting is created in the imagination of the reader in light and form, shadow and line; and the very atmosphere of Shut-in Valley and Ironside with the mountains isolating the people who live in their shadows, or Queenborough and Mulberry Street with all their human associations become alive. Language which can evoke this awareness is effective; and it is such language that creates *Vein of Iron*.

II *In This Our* Life

In This Our Life (1941) was written under the great difficulties attendant upon Ellen Glasgow's serious illness; but her book, in spite of such a hindrance, is remarkable for beauty and clarity of style and for force in narration and character portrayal. Miss Glasgow suspected that this might be her last novel; she tried to make it as fine a book as she had ever written.

When she began writing *In This Our Life*, she set the opening scenes in 1935; however, when she had completed the first draft and begun the second writing, she felt it advisable to move the time of the action to 1938. The span of the book reaches, therefore, from the spring of 1938, when Stanley Timberlake is about to be married, until August, 1939, on the eve of World War II. The setting in place for Ellen Glasgow's drama of happiness-hunters and of others who despair of happiness in this existence and are willing to settle with God or Destiny for a little quiet and peace is Richmond—thinly disguised as Queenborough. But in this book, Miss Glasgow made less effort to suggest that her imagined Virginia town was other than the city in which she lived.

Because Ellen Glasgow wished to present the "interior life of a community," she so designed her novel that the "outlook would be more diffused than individual. . . ." She thought of her problem as "an analysis in fiction of the modern temper . . . a dissolving moment in time . . . one of those perpetually returning epochs, which fall between an age that is slipping out and an age that is hastening in."[1] She thought that she interpreted in her novel "the intrinsic life of a community, as portrayed through the group consciousness. . . ."; that her theme was revealed as "the conflict of human beings with human nature, of civilization with biology."[2]

The action of the novel presents Asa Timberlake and his family during the culminating events in their assorted dramas of pretense and frustration. Asa, who has known a mean life, sees little hope of a better one. He is fifty-nine years old, and for forty-seven of these years he has been a drudge in the tobacco factory which had once belonged to his family but which now belongs to a large corporation. His wearing toil, his inadequate pay, and his miserable existence with a wife whom he dislikes and who delights in tormenting him have been Asa's life.

Stanley Timberlake, Asa's and Lavinia's spoiled, pretty daughter is about to be married to Craig Fleming, a young lawyer. Shortly before the wedding should have taken place, she runs off with Peter Kingsmill, her sister Roy's surgeon husband. Roy, hurt but refusing to surrender to her injury, gives Peter his freedom through divorce and continues her work in an interior decorating shop. Craig Fleming, made of softer stuff, gives way to despair and drink until he and Roy strike up a friendship which ripens into love—or so they believe.

Asa, meanwhile, continues his mean existence with his hypochondriac, pseudo-invalid wife Lavinia. He finds his only gleam of brightness in an occasional Sunday afternoon with Kate Oliver at her farm, "Hunter's Fare." He longs for the day when Lavinia's Uncle William Fitzroy will die, bequeath her enough money to make her independent, and free him so he can leave.

The marriage of the happiness-hunters, Peter and Stanley, becomes their source of misery; Peter, who can no longer live with Stanley or himself, eventually commits suicide. Stanley returns to Queenborough. Hitherto, Stanley has been able to twist Uncle William as she pleased; but now he is no longer the lustful old tycoon who had spoiled her. He is occupied with his own problem; for he has learned that he must soon die of cancer and the knowledge terrifies him.

Stanley, trying to escape from herself, seeks the anodyne of speed in the fast sports car old William had given her. One evening she runs over and kills a child, drives away from the scene of the accident, leaves her car, and comes home. Later, when the police investigate, she lets them think that Parry Clay, a young colored boy who had been looking after the car, had been driving it that evening. Parry is, of course, tossed into the Queenborough jail. Shielded by the pretense and sentiment of Lavinia, by Uncle William and his wife, Charlotte, and, once more, by Craig Fleming, Stanley seems well protected. Asa, however, detects the flaws in his daughter's story and forces her to tell the truth. Parry is freed from the physical confinement of the jail, but he can never be freed from the humiliation and injustice of his treatment. Stanley, of course, with the aid of Uncle William and her status as a white lady, escapes punishment.

Roy Timberlake, who had planned to marry Craig, now realizes that he has never escaped from his sentimental fascination for her sister. Roy breaks her engagement with him, goes out into the rainy night, and encounters a young Englishman who is as lost as she. She goes with him to an apartment where she gives him the comfort of her body and her spirit. Although she returns to her home the next morning, she does so only to get her clothes; she plans to leave Queenborough.

Asa cannot prevent her departure; he knows that he cannot change these lives. He does hope that he can find some peace, for he knows that old William has already settled sufficient money on Lavinia to make it possible for her to live comfortably without him. He intends to give up his place in the tobacco factory and go to "Hunter's Fare" to work as Kate Oliver's hired man; Queenborough and Lavinia may think what they wish.

Both *In This Our Life* and *The Sheltered Life* treat the evils of sham, of happiness-hunters, and of dangerous selfishness masquerading as innocence. The earlier novel, however, moved with a lightness of touch illuminated by a style and tone very different from the ironic thrusts and the stylistic brilliance of *In This Our Life*. In *The Sheltered Life* and in the two preceding comedies of manners, as well as in *Vein of Iron*, Ellen Glasgow interpreted human lives with a mockery, sometime stinging, often cutting, yet rarely mortal in its thrusts; but for *In This Our Life* she used a sharper, crueler pen. Her ironic view darkens to a bitterly sardonic tone, but her bitterness she in part modified with a pity for all tormented mortals conveyed through Asa Timberlake.

Ellen Glasgow has no sympathy with others of her characters, for Lavinia Timberlake is one of the most insufferably repulsive creations ever encountered in the pages of fiction. She is selfish, soft, sentimental, and cruel—but she is by no means a fool. She had been an unattractive young girl who had persuaded Asa Timberlake that he was in love with her. His temporary infatuation had not long survived a few months of marriage; but they had lived over thirty years in loveless propinquity and had three children. Lavinia had found chronic invalidism and a life in bed the best means of tyrannizing over Asa and of usually gaining her own way.

William Fitzroy, like old Cyrus Treadwell of *Virginia*, is a "great man" in Queenborough because he has acquired power through money; what he says and does seem important because he is rich. His money enables Lavinia to live in a new house (which Asa despises) and to avoid the penury which would otherwise result from Asa's small wages. Old Uncle William has spoiled Stanley because of his lecherous, more than avuncular interest in his full-lipped, bright-haired niece who early learned how to wheedle gifts from him. Roy, the older sister, receives less of his attention, for she will not prostitute herself to his attentions. All in all, William Fitzroy is a wonderfully repulsive portrait of an avaricious, ruthless, insensitive, yet sentimental Southern man of affairs. He may keep platinum blonde mistresses in New York, but he is a faithful worshiper at the Episcopal Church in Queenborough, and he also makes pious utterances about religion.

Peter Kingsmill and Craig Fleming represent two aspects of modern youth. Peter possesses the surgeon's hands but not his temperament. He is a shallow young man of great physical charm who has no depth of mind or spirit. Why should Roy Timberlake love him? The answer may be as simple as why Asa, her father, married Lavinia: in love and marriage human beings rarely act logically or reasonably. Peter, fascinated by Stanley Timberlake, goes off with her; but he cannot support her as she wishes to be kept. Desperate over his financial affairs and his miserable life with Stanley, he drinks, endangers his work at the hospital, and kills himself. Beneath his handsome exterior he possessed a conscience with which he could no longer live.

Stanley Timberlake is young, flashily attractive, and completely self-centered. She has been able to twist men and sentimental women around her finger since she was an infant because she was so "sweet" in appearance, so innocent looking. Her innocence masks an insidious evil quality more dangerous than poison. She is completely amoral; her only governing influence is desire. If she wants something, then she must have it. When she runs down a small child, she knows no remorse, only fear of punishment.

Ellen Glasgow realized that girls such as Stanley walked the best streets of Queenborough and lived in the most "sheltered" homes. In these pages she revealed Stanley as she would appear to the unseeing eye—a pretty, even beautiful, occasionally petulant, often charming girl, dressed in the fashion of her time, seeking the inconsequential amusements of her day. But Ellen Glasgow also removed from Stanley her bright surface.

Craig Fleming is Ellen Glasgow's modern young radical without the spiritual stamina, or, as old William Fitzroy would say, the guts to act. Craig is interested in all sorts of liberal movements, but he is a weak reed for Roy or anyone else to lean upon. He feels that Roy has rescued him from himself and despair, and he tries to persuade her to marry him on the grounds that he needs her. Roy, however, is weary of being "needed."

Roy Timberlake is strong in most of the ways in which Peter, Craig, and Stanley are weak or vicious. She refuses to grieve or hate when she is deserted by Peter; instead she buys a red hat and keeps on with her work. She sees through her mother and her sister, and she is the only one of the family who recognizes the utterly mean life her father has lived. Almost the last thing she says near the end of the novel is: ". . . I want something to hold by! I want something good!"[3] Roy Timberlake represents Ellen Glasgow's vision of a member of the younger generation who may find salvation when others are lost.

Asa's and Lavinia's son, Andrew, and his wife, Maggie, are the symbols of complete mediocrity. In the very emptiness of their souls they constitute a sharp condemnation of average Americans. Because they represent so many, they symbolize the terrible danger of their thoughtless unawareness of what surrounds them. Their innocence carries its poison too.

The colored family of the Clays—Abel, Minerva, and their son, Parry—receives special attention in this novel. Their lives and the tragic destruction of Parry symbolize the terrible situation of the respectable colored family in America. An employee of the Post Office, Abel owns a small home where he raises flowers and Minerva washes and irons for white families. Their son, Parry, is bright, has done well in school, and aspires to further

education and a career as a lawyer. He seeks aid from old
William Fitzroy, but that old aristocrat turns him away because
he believes there are enough white lawyers to take care of
Negroes. If Parry can read, write, and do sums, that is sufficient.
Although Parry is eventually assured of aid from Craig Fleming,
they reckon without thought of Parry's skin. When the boy
comes out of the jail after his unjust arrest and his abuse as
a Negro prisoner, his ambitions to raise himself may never
overcome the experience of being once more reminded that he,
as a Negro, must expect a different brand of justice—a different
life, a limited opportunity.

Ellen Glasgow shows that the Clays are very light-skinned
Negroes who have some Indian and much white blood. Parry
is so light that he might easily "pass" in the North. As a younger
Negro, he, however, is proud of his Negro race—though he is
probably more white than black. Ironically, Craig Fleming, to
the shocked anger of old William Fitzroy, questions just *what*
is Parry's race. In contrast to Craig's attitude is another contained
in a most telling passage in which Minerva replies to Asa's
question as to whether she had told the police that Parry had
been with her on the night of the accident: "I told 'em, Mr. Asa,
. . . But they wouldn't believe me. I'm colored."[4]

Asa Timberlake is the last of Ellen Glasgow's "civilized"
human beings. A failure in the eyes of his wife and Uncle
William because he has never made money, he is understood
for his true worth only by Roy, by Kate Oliver, and, possibly,
by Craig Fleming. No saint, he not only dislikes but despises
Lavinia; he is the most thoroughly human and outwardly unheroic
hero of all of Ellen Glasgow's civilized men. A quiet unobtrusive
hero, Asa blends into the backgrounds of many scenes when
the more noisy, shallow, or vicious individuals are making themselves seen and heard. Ellen Glasgow reveals him to the ob-
servant reader; she may have failed to make him clear, for all
his value, to the less perceptive.

He has endured the attrition of a mean existence without
losing his humanity or his sense of humor; he has learned to
observe the antics of his world with ironic amusement; and, in
a sense, he has won a certain freedom of the spirit through
irony rather than despair. He is still bound by his sense of
responsibility, his heritage from his well-born mother and father.
Hence, he stays with Lavinia as long as she needs him. On the

other hand, he is not blinded by any false notions of propriety. When he knows that his wife is independent and can have a nurse instead of him, he has no hesitation about going to "Hunter's Fare" for a few years of decency and happiness.

Asa's intended escape to "Hunter's Fare" should not be misunderstood, therefore, as an agrarian retreat from industrialism, for he does not condemn life; he wishes to escape not only from a bad life but to have the kind of work he has always desired. More than that, living on the farm with Kate Oliver will mean the companionship—even love of a sort—which he has missed through most of his existence. Asa's departure from the city is a very personal act and not a symbol of agrarianism.

Throughout *In This Our Life* an atmosphere of impending as well as of present evil moves through the pages like a dark cloud. Not only is there the tone of change but also the awareness of some shadowy danger hovering near. The characters live at the end of an age and before another has filled its place. Ellen Glasgow, writing just before World War II and during the first years of that conflict, evoked the atmosphere of those times. She suggested that, for most human beings in the fourth decade of the twentieth century, human nature is too powerful to make possible the existence of the civilized person who is "genuine," who refuses shams, and who seeks a good life which is his own and not the ready-made set of reactions and inhibitions turned out by a money-dominated society in the name of a "way of life."

An air of illness also pervades *In This Our Life*. This is presented in Lavinia's invalid existence, her demands on Asa to serve her as a nurse, her medicines and doctors; in Peter's suicide and in Stanley's subsequent "convalescence"; and in old William's cancer. But this odor of decay and dissolution is more than physical; for Ellen Glasgow suggests a sick society through Lavinia, who has learned how to use her pseudo-invalidism as a weapon; through Old William, who refuses to learn the truth about his cancer until it is too late; and through Stanley's keyed-up, mad drive toward the destruction not only of herself but of all who come within her range. Only Asa and Roy have acquired some protection against the miasma which these people breathe—a bad air peculiar not only to their lives but also to American society. Asa and Roy are at least in some degree civilized; the others are not.

Although it may be thought that *In This Our Life* is an unpleasant book, it is not. It is a very serious book, but it is neither
despairing nor morbid. The excellence of the writing, as well
as the strength of Asa and Roy, offsets the dark evil of other
features of the novel. Though the tone of the book is sombre,
it is frequently illuminated by flashes of light. To achieve these
effects, the method of narration is well chosen. Usually analytical,
cool, ironic, clear, and objective, this approach and this cool
attitude are contrasted with warmth of feeling such as is found
in the sections revealing Asa or the Negro family.

Readers surprised by *The Woman Within*, should have read
In This Our Life more carefully. Ellen Glasgow's troubled vision
of life in her late years is evident in this last novel, but it is not
finally a despairing conclusion to which she brings herself and
her characters Asa and Roy. Into this book Ellen Glasgow
poured her pity, her malice, her hatred of sham, her longing for
the strength she lacked, her hatred of cruelty, her search for
values, and her yearning, with Roy Timberlake, for something
good to hold by.

In her final essay in *A Certain Measure* Ellen Glasgow
discussed *In This Our Life*, her last published novel. She had
tried to present "an analysis in fiction of the modern temper, . . .
confused, vacillating, uncertain, and distracted from permanent
values."[5] She emphasized the idea that Asa Timberlake "mirrors
the tragedy of a social system which lives, grows, and prospers
by material standards alone."[6] She thought that the novel came
to a pause and not to an end, and she regretted that its essential
meanings had not been clearly understood. For these reasons
she said that she would write another novel "of Asa's hard-won
freedom"; this was with meaning called *Beyond Defeat*.[7]

III *Beyond Defeat*

The short sequel which Ellen Glasgow wrote after *In This
Our Life* may never be published. She had decided not to
publish it because she was unable to bring it to the final form
she desired. Some comment on what she wrote in this book
may be of interest to readers of *In This Our Life*.

The novel covers the events on the day of Roy's return to
Queenborough after an absence of several years. In this period
she has borne the son conceived by the young, unknown

Englishman with whom she slept on that last night related in *In This Our Life*. Roy and her son represent the possibility of the future in an allegorical and symbolical narrative. The elders have made a mess of things, but Roy and her son out of the Unknown supposedly hold the keys to a new kingdom. Much of this allegory is too hazy to be effective, and Ellen Glasgow realized it.

In the sequel she also tells of Asa's departure to "Hunter's Fare" even though Lavinia and her friends are (or pretend to be) shocked at this violation of polite pretenses. Lavinia has been living very comfortably on her income from the money bequeathed her by her Uncle William. Lavinia dies—her doing so might have pleased the readers and made the book worth while; that and Asa's real happiness. Though unsatisfactory in the state in which Ellen Glasgow left it, *Beyond Defeat* does clarify some points which she believed had been misunderstood in *In This Our Life,* especially with respect to Asa and Roy Timberlake and their significance.

CHAPTER 10

A Final Word

I *Critical Reception—1897 to 1925*

FROM 1897, with the publication of *The Descendant,* Ellen Glasgow received serious and often favorable critical attention. She was not singled out as a youthful genius, but her work was noticed and her promise of greater achievement discerned by reviewers and critics. Hamlin Garland was among the few critics of her first novel who perceived the promising qualities in the young author.[1] A reviewer in *The Critic* shrewdly guessed that the author was a woman, compared the novel favorably with the work of Sir Hall Caine, and admired the writing of the book and its human interest.[2] Although published when the most popular fiction was the historical romance or the adventure story, *The Descendant* surprisingly went into three editions.[3]

Although *Phases of an Inferior Planet* (1898), Ellen Glasgow's second published novel, received mixed notices, *The Voice of the People* (1900) received more perceptive critical attention. Reviewers spoke of the "unflinching realism and unfailing sympathy" with which the "agony of the poor white trash" was portrayed and of the "all-pervading humor which plays over the surface of the narrative."[4] Some thought it well written and interesting.[5]

The Battle-Ground (1902) received generally a more favorable reception than had Ellen Glasgow's previous novels. Hamilton Wright Mabie, a leading literary journalist, spoke of its lack of melodrama, grandiloquence, and sentimentality, and he thought that the author ranked with Thomas Nelson Page and Joel Chandler Harris in her handling of the Negro dialect.[6] A critic in *World's Work,* who may have been Walter Hines Page, its editor, said: "She is not a 'Southern' writer nor a 'Northern'

writer, but a writer of human life as it develops itself every-
where under the conditions that her stories naturally find. She
has understood and practiced this law of the best writing and
escaped the snare of provinciality. . . ."[7]

Such critical understanding Ellen Glasgow sought all through
her career but rarely found. Too many critics near the turn of
the century could see little beyond the sincerity and charm of
her novels. In a year when Owen Wister's *The Virginian* and
Alice Hegan Rice's *Mrs. Wiggs of the Cabbage Patch* dominated
American fiction, *The Battle-Ground* sold well. It was the first
novel Ellen Glasgow had written which seemed to belong to
the then popular genre of historical fiction, but she had written
it with artistry and good taste.[8]

The Deliverance (1904) won a reception which showed Ellen
Glasgow more popular with the reading public but still "not . . .
accorded consistent or lasting acclaim as a first ranking author
of the day."[9] Though she gained readers and received some
praise from Southern reviewers, she had not succeeded in proving
how she differed from the popular romancers of the time.[10] In
England the reviews were generally complimentary but not
very penetrating. It appears, however, that by 1904 Ellen Glasgow
was "fairly widely read in England."[11] Though her critics had
considered her above the ordinary, she felt that her production
had not kept pace with her ability.[12]

The Wheel of Life (1906) elicited a mixed reception and
did not improve Ellen Glasgow's literary reputation, for some
critics believed that she was yielding to the popular fashion
in fiction.[13] Most of those who found *The Ancient Law* (1908)
an improvement over her earlier work revealed their limited
knowledge of her other novels. Others used their reviews to
appraise her over-all achievement in fiction. By some Northern
critics she was still considered a novelist of the Southern
romantic school.

The Romance of a Plain Man (1909) drew more appreciative
comment than had the two books which had preceded it. *The
New York Times* praised the author's powers of observation and
description, much of her characterization, and her instinct for
the dramatic situation and the telling phrase.[14] When *The Miller
of Old Church* appeared in 1911, most reviews were favorable.
The North American Review compared her work in this book
with that of Thomas Hardy in her feeling for the land and in

her creation of rustic characters.[15] *The New York Times* said: "Among American novelists of the present there is none who excels Ellen Glasgow in portrayal of character and in rich humanity of background."[16]

Virginia (1913) seems to have been considered by its reviewers Ellen Glasgow's best novel up to that time. Its readers, however, did not favor it so strongly.[17] *Life and Gabriella* (1916) enjoyed considerable popular success. Many but not all of the reviewers thought well of the novel;[18] *The New York Times* observed the author's "artistic conscientiousness" and her "subtlety and finesse."[19] *The Nation,* however, vigorously condemned the novel and its author for verbosity and obviousness.[20] *The Builders* (1919) received relatively little attention and that often unfavorable. And her next novel, *One Man in His Time* (1922) did nothing to advance Ellen Glasgow's reputation. *The Shadowy Third and Other Stories* (1923) received little attention, although *The Literary Review* commented on the fine construction and craftsmanship of the stories.[21]

From 1911 to 1925 Ellen Glasgow received attention from several critics who considered her over-all achievement. Joyce Kilmer, now remembered as the author of "Trees," published an essay in which he recorded that Ellen Glasgow had told him that "evasive idealism" was what was wrong with American literature.[22] Carl Van Doren commented at some length on Ellen Glasgow's work in his *Contemporary American Novelists, 1900-1920* in which, although he persisted in thinking of her as belonging to the older school of Southern romancers and local color, he did recognize values in *Virginia.*[23] Louise Maunsell Field, writing of her in 1923, spoke of Ellen Glasgow's "quiet humour spiced with delicate irony, humour of insight and character more closely akin to Jane Austen's than to that of any other writer."[24] Dr. Joseph Collins said that ". . . In style she has no superior and few peers amongst [sic] the fiction writers of the day in this country. . . . She has the gift of character delineation and she has learned how to give value to perspective."[25]

II *1925–1941*

With *Barren Ground* (1925) Ellen Glasgow achieved a place of even higher esteem with both critics and the general reader. Widely and usually favorably reviewed, the novel was named on the *Review of Reviews*' list of twenty-five outstanding novels of the year; and in the group was Lewis' *Arrowsmith,* Edith Wharton's *The Mother's Recompense,* Edna Ferber's *So Big,* Willa Cather's *The Professor's House,* and Sherwood Anderson's *Dark Laughter.*[26] Because the publishers spoke in their advertising of *Barren Ground* as representing "realism crossing the Potomac," this attitude was reflected by some of the more ignorant reviewers. But Stuart Pratt Sherman refuted this notion, saying:

> She was a realist when some of our popular exponents of realism were in the cradle. She preceded into the field Mrs. Wharton who is twelve years older and Mr. Dreiser who is three years older. . . . Her democratic fighting realism is already incarnate in the little redhaired hero of 'The Voice of the People,' 1900. Realism crossed the Potomac twenty-five years ago, going North.[27]

Mr. Sherman pointed out that Ellen Glasgow had treated "provincial life from a national point of view . . . critically and with a surgical use of satire." He praised "her clear sense of the elemental things in human life and her sense of the profound interdependence of man and nature," and he spoke of her style as "firm, lucid and [having] masculine rhythms."[28] Critics in *The Atlantic Monthly*[29] and *The Virginia Quarterly Review*[30] praised *Barren Ground* for its emphasis on values and its truth to life.

The Romantic Comedians (1926) not only received wide critical approval but created a sensation in Richmond, where many residents thought they recognized its relevance to the author's one-time love affair and long friendship with Henry Anderson. Carl Van Vechten spoke of Ellen Glasgow's "malicious feminine wit [which] hovers over this volume as beneficently as the redolent bouquet of fine champagne 1812 rises from the depths of a crystal goblet."[31] When *They Stooped to Folly* (1929) appeared, it received a mingled but generally favorable reception from both critics and book buyers. Its reception was a friendly one both in the South and in England; and H. L. Mencken, hitherto cool to Ellen Glasgow's work, came around to her side.[32]

From the early 1930's Ellen Glasgow received more attention as a front-rank American author to be compared with Edith Wharton, Willa Cather, Theodore Dreiser, and Sinclair Lewis. James Branch Cabell, Ellen Glasgow's long-time friend and usually friendly, if sometimes acid, critic, thought that serious critical recognition had come late to the Virginia novelist

because her early works had been written under the influence
of the kind of fiction which had been fashionable in the latter
decades of the nineteenth century. These modes had changed,
and the merits of her earlier novels had been hidden from later
readers. Cabell thought that her earlier readers had found her
work stolid and wholesome, but he objected to what he thought
to be their too great length, sentiment, dialect, and sometimes
forced happy endings.[33]

In spite of, or because of, the criticism it received, *The
Sheltered Life* (1932) brought Ellen Glasgow to her highest
point in recognition and popularity. The book stood fifth on
the best-seller lists. Yet once more the Pulitzer Prize selectors
passed over an Ellen Glasgow novel, and the author had the
dubious pleasure of the consolations of her friends among critics
and other readers. *Vein of Iron* (1935), though not so enthusiastically received as *The Sheltered Life,* added to Ellen Glasgow's
reputation in America. It received little attention in England.
Much of the reviewing was perceptive as well as favorable, but
it was still possible for well-meaning critics to misread a Glasgow
novel.

In This Our Life, Ellen Glasgow's last published novel,
appeared in March, 1941. Howard Mumford Jones admired the
book as a "product of the tragic muse."[34] *Time* magazine gave
considerable space to a review of the novel, observing with
admirable insight that Ellen Glasgow's "novels are no more
provincially Virginian than 'The Trojan Women' is Trojan. Their
major theme is human struggle, and Novelist Glasgow broods
over her foredoomed characters with irony, pity and passion,
but without sentimentality."[35] James Southall Wilson, out of his
knowledge of her achievement, wrote in praise of "the charm of
Ellen Glasgow's witty prose" and her "practical artist's skill."
He spoke further of *In This Our Life* as possessing ease of
reading, spice, daring and beauty of style, vivid characterization;
as offering "a challenge to this generation," and as raising
"questions to be pondered over for tomorrow."[36] *In This Our
Life* was awarded the Pulitzer Prize as the best fiction for
1941—perhaps more as belated recognition of the worth of
Ellen Glasgow as novelist than for the excellence of her novel.

In the fifteen years from 1926 to 1941, other critical opinion
of the work of Ellen Glasgow appeared in critical articles and
passages in books of literary history and criticism. Professor

Edwin Mims admired her novels for their treatment of the role of women in society.[37] Grant Overton spoke of Ellen Glasgow's writing of a life for women in which love need not be paramount, of her interpretation of the Southern middle class, of her knowledge of the limitations of men, and of her epigrams and her irony.[38]

When James Southall Wilson reviewed the Old Dominion Edition of Ellen Glasgow's novels in 1933, he thought that *The Sheltered Life* had been too good to win a Pultizer Prize but that *The Romantic Comedians* was perfect in its kind. He wrote:

> . . . A compassionate sense of the tragedy of life gives an ironic flavor to her comedy of manners which makes its wit more biting, without turning bitter the kindliness of her tolerance. . . . Above all, her wit is forever fresh—with an epigrammatic tang that makes everything she writes delightful.[39]

When the *Virginia Edition of the Works of Ellen Glasgow* was published in 1938, it was reviewed extensively. Henry Seidel Canby and J. Donald Adams availed themselves of the opportunity to assess Ellen Glasgow's over-all achievement. Mr. Canby saw the novelist in the great classical tradition of the novel of manners and nominated her "as our best contemporary master of the tragic drama of significant manners" and "as our tenderest realist of men (men more than women), and our most clear-eyed ironist, for since she is ironic only of the men and women she likes and admires, she never mixes her irony with the stronger but cruder brew of satire."[40] Mr. Adams compared Ellen Glasgow's interest in the technique of the art of fiction to that of Henry James. He praised her depiction of old men such as General Archbald in *The Sheltered Life*. He thought this novel and *Barren Ground* were novels "with timeless themes, without the least dependence on 'trends' in the novel, . . ."[41]

Herschel Brickell in 1941 compared Ellen Glasgow and John P. Marquand. He found points of comparison in their ironical detachment, their affectionate understanding of their own people and their own parts of the world, their aloofness and perspective in their treatment of their material, the influence of their environments upon them, their well-bred attitude toward life, the fact that they both wrote of a dying class, and the fact that they had both done their best work in middle age. He thought the conservatism in method of both writers especially note-worthy.[42] But Professor Joseph Warren Beach frowned on Ellen Glasgow for what he characterized as "her long expositions, her formal characterizations, her perpetual perfunctory land-scapes, and above all her endless colorless records of what her characters think and feel on all occasions."[43]

III   A Certain Measure (1943), The Woman Within (1954)

In This Our Life completed the roll of Ellen Glasgow's published novels, but in 1943 she brought out A Certain Measure, her last book published in her lifetime. This book of criticism received wide praise. Hamilton Basso wrote a long review of the book for The New York Times Book Review in which he emphasized her importance in depicting the rise of the middle classes in post-Civil War America, her achievement as one not provincially Southern, her membership in Thomas Jefferson's natural aristocracy of talent and virtue, her high standards in art, and her opposition to literary commercialism.[44]

The years which followed Ellen Glasgow's death in 1945 witnessed some decline in interest in her work. Until recently her novels, with the exceptions of Barren Ground and Vein of Iron, have not been readily available. True, theses and disserta-tions have been written upon her work, and she has been ac-corded respectful notice in works of literary history and criticism.

Henry Seidel Canby wrote rather coolly of her in The Literary History of the United States (1948). George F. Whicher gave some attention to her in The Literature of the American People (1951). Van Wyck Brooks wrote enthusiastically in his The Confident Years (1952). And Edward Wagenknecht in his Cavalcade of the American Novel (1952) provided a favorable if somewhat inaccurate account of her career. Articles concerning Ellen Glasgow by John Hardy and by me appeared in Southern Renascence . . . (1953); Mr. Hardy was caustically hostile while I, perhaps naturally, was more favorable. Maxwell Geismar, in Rebels and Ancestors (1953), provided, a generally sound analysis of Ellen Glasgow's fiction, except for his rather surprisingly high estimate of The Wheel of Life. Professor Jay B. Hubbell in his The South in American Literature (1954) recognized

Ellen Glasgow's importance in Southern writing as well as in the broader range of American letters.

When *The Woman Within* appeared in 1954, it excited some interested and often puzzled reactions. Yet the comments about this book did not suggest a greatly revived critical interest in her novels. The same reaction could have been observed when my edition of the letters of Ellen Glasgow was published in 1958. The interest of the reviewers was more in what the letters revealed about the personality of the author than in their pertinence for a clearer understanding of her fiction.

Writing in *The New York Times Book Review* in 1955, J. Donald Adams commented on Ellen Glasgow ten years after her death:

> While I do not place Ellen Glasgow among the world's greatest novelists . . . I do rank her among the best we Americans have produced. In one respect she stands pre-eminent. She is the wittiest novelist in our history, bar none, and one of the best stylists. . . . Willa Cather was her superior in some respects, but she had neither wit nor humor, and Miss Glasgow had both.
>
> .   .   .   .   .   .
>
> Too much, perhaps, has been made of her role as a satirical critic of the Southern society into which she was born; that was one of her important functions as an American novelist—her exposure of the South's romantic tradition; but it is my belief that she will be remembered longer for her deeply considered reading of the human heart, studied by accident in the milieu she knew best, for her understanding of the age-old conflict between youth and age, and of the never-ending battle between the sexes.[45]

As Ellen Glasgow looked back upon more than half a century of writing, she felt that she had never received the recognition which she and her fiction deserved. Most of her books had sold well, but she had sought a reputation not based upon "best seller" values but upon the esteem of a body of discriminating readers and critics. Actually, she won this esteem to a far greater degree than she admitted.

Ellen Glasgow thought that she had been ahead of her times and something of a radical when she began her career. She also felt that later times caught up with her and moved on in paths and directions she did not care to tread. She felt that she was as radical or as conservative as in her youth, that at least she was in the company of those who aspired to being "civilized"—a state neither new or old, radical or conservative, but universal and eternal for those who attain it.

IV *Critic of the Sterile, Monstrous Life*

Ellen Glasgow changed in her attitude toward the South and things Southern, but not as some of her critics have supposed. She had castigated the evils and weaknesses of Southern society in her youth; she continued to scorn weakness and folly all through her career. If she saw the South of her later years as less than utopian, she did not look back with longing to an ante-bellum, heroic age. General Archbald, one of her "civilized" men, had gone against the current of his youth—a time hostile to the values cherished by the General and the novelist. Asa Timberlake, a few years younger than his author, did not look back with longing upon his childhood and youth. Ellen Glasgow's castigation of "modern" times has been carelessly misunderstood. Actually, she condemned whatever she found in the life of men and women which made those lives barren, sterile, and monstrous. She was aware of the tragedy involved in the waste of human potentialities in any age and in any level of society.

Ellen Glasgow was a follower neither of the industrialism of the "new South" of her youth nor of the new conservatism which called itself agrarianism in her mature years. Her delight in nature and her interest in the possibilities of life on the land have been misunderstood as expressions of agrarian doctrine. She once indicated her attitude in these matters when she observed that, although she had no love for the dirt and odors of industry, neither did she care for hookworm and pellagra—the too common features of poor Southern rural existence. Where her Southern agrarian contemporaries sketched a return to a Southern pastoral-agricultural golden age, Ellen Glasgow looked hard at the actualities of Southern rural life with its poverty, disease, and spiritually inhibiting elements.

She knew that many of these undesirable conditions could be changed, and she indicated the possibilities of change through the working of intelligence and character, as in Dorinda Oakley. If she attacked the evils of a commercial, materialistic culture calling itself civilization, she did not offer agrarianism as her

formula for the attaining of man's hopes. Ultimately, she explored
the possible answers to these questions: wherein lies the good
life, in what can man find his greatest reward, in what manner
of life can he live as a truly civilized human being? The
answers, she knew, lay within the individual, not specifically in
town or country, nor in a set of magic formulae.

Though Ellen Glasgow could speak scornfully of Southern
purveyors of horror tales masquerading as realism, she had more
in common with at least one of her younger Southern contemporaries than she may have realized. In a large degree she had
pioneered in the treatment of Southern material which William
Faulkner later utilized. Her Virginia poor whites are usually
treated more sympathetically than Faulkner's Mississippi lower
classes. If there are no Snopeses in Ellen Glasgow's pages,
there are some near relations to that despicable clan. Old Rainy
Day Jones in *The Battle-Ground* would have recognized a cousin
in Ab Snopes of *The Unvanquished*. Both Ellen Glasgow and
Faulkner were aware of the problems of the lower-class Southern
white man in his struggle to better himself economically and
socially.

Like Faulkner, Ellen Glasgow treated her Southern aristocrat
with mixed admiration and regret. She, like her younger contemporary, recognized the worth of the aristocratic individual at
his best, as well as the fallacies and weaknesses of his manner
of life and his beliefs when they had ceased to be supported by
individual strength of character. Throughout her fiction she
castigated the aristocratic pretense which served only as a mask
for lives empty of values.

Like Faulkner later, if less violently, she condemned waste
of material values, but even more did she condemn the waste
and destruction of the human spirit. She sought imaginatively
to discover and define the civilized human being as, in his
rather different way, William Faulkner found his in Uncle Ike
McCaslin or V. K. Ratliff. Those Faulkner heroes of the truth
world find much in common with Uncle Tucker Corbin of
The Deliverance, General Archbald of *The Sheltered Life*, John
Fincastle of *Vein of Iron*, and Asa Timberlake of *In This Our Life*.

Like William Faulkner, Ellen Glasgow recognized the worth
of the Southern Negro. She never used her Negro characters
for low comedy or sentimental effects. She saw them and
understood them as persons of significance in their own right.

William Faulkner's Dilsey of *The Sound and the Fury* would have found a sister in Aunt Mehitable of *Barren Ground* in wisdom and enduring character. His Sam Fathers of *The Bear* might have found much in common with Big Abel of *The Battle-Ground* or with some of the Negroes who were Dorinda Oakley's neighbors and helpers in *Barren Ground*.

If William Faulkner has seemed to speak more forcefully, even violently, in his treatment of Southern mores and problems than did Ellen Glasgow, we should not overlook Ellen Glasgow's willingness to speak harshly where she found it necessary. Old Cyrus Treadwell in *Virginia,* with his coldly cynical disregard for his yellow one-time concubine and their son, may compare easily with Faulkner's treatment of white-Negro relations. And there are few chapters in William Faulkner's most revolting portrayals of human degradation to compare with Ellen Glasgow's old Dr. Greylock and his tribe of yellow children, or with Jason Greylock's ultimate destruction. If Ellen Glasgow spoke with more decorum, she spoke no less plainly, even violently, of the darker side of human existence.

Both the older Southern writer and her younger contemporary, Faulkner, wrote of Southern men and women as they saw and understood them; she of Virginians, he of Mississippians, but both fundamentally of the essential human being. Both evince concern with ultimate human values and the measurement of man by those values.

Notes and References

Chapter One

1. Some of the materials upon which the chronology and the biographical portions of this book are based will be found in *A Certain Measure, The Woman Within,* and *Letters of Ellen Glasgow.* Other materials are in unpublished papers and correspondence in the Glasgow Collection and other collections in the Alderman Library of the University of Virginia; in materials pertaining to Ellen Glasgow gathered by the late Marjorie Kinnan Rawlings and left in the care of her literary executor, Mrs. Julia S. Bigham; and in the Glasgow letters and notes which I have collected from libraries and from private individuals who had known the novelist.

2. A letter from Dr. Joseph Collins, New York physician and amateur literary critic, suggests that he had known the physician whom the novelist loved. Comments in the M. K. Rawlings papers suggest that others also believed that this or another physician may have been "Gerald B——." Though somewhat persuasive, none of this is conclusive evidence for a certain identification.

3. Henry W. Anderson's letters to Ellen Glasgow are in the Glasgow papers in the Alderman Library of the University of Virginia. Ellen Glasgow's letters to Mr. Anderson have not survived.

4. This speech is among the manuscripts in the Glasgow papers in the Alderman Library at the University of Virginia.

5. *Letters of Ellen Glasgow,* ed. Blair Rouse (New York, 1958), p. 151.

6. *Ibid.,* p. 104.

7. *Ibid.,* p. 261.

8. In addition to using Ellen Glasgow's autobiographical volumes and her letters, I have drawn upon a paper on the novelist's reading prepared by her nephew, Col. C. C. Tutwiler.

9. Ellen Glasgow, *A Certain Measure* (New York, 1943), p. 16.

10. *Ibid.*

11. See note 4 above.

Chapter Two

1. Ellen Glasgow, *The Woman Within* (New York, 1954), p. 41.

2. *Letters of Ellen Glasgow,* p. 268 (August 2, 1940).

3. *Ibid.,* p. 211 (April 28, 1936).

4. *Ibid.*

5. *Ibid.*, p. 159 (July 28, 1934).

6. *Ibid.*, pp. 369-70.

7. Glasgow, *A Certain Measure*, p. 104 (Probably written in 1937 or 1938).

8. *Ibid.*, p. 30.

9. *Ibid.*, pp. 260-61.

10. *Letters of Ellen Glasgow*, p. 124 (September 22, 1932).

11. *Ibid.*, p. 335 (October 24, 1943; Professor Jones's review appeared in *The Saturday Review of Literature*, October 16, 1943.).

12. *Ibid.*, pp. 163-64.

13. *Ibid.*, p. 14.

14. *Ibid.*, p. 116.

15. *Ibid.*, p. 148.

16. *Ibid.*, p. 24.

17. Glasgow, *A Certain Measure*, p. 28.

18. *Ibid.*

19. I visited Ellen Glasgow at her home in Richmond on December 19, 1941, and talked with her at some length about her life and work. This conversation will be referred to hereafter as "Interview with Ellen Glasgow."

20. Glasgow, *A Certain Measure*, pp. 48-50.

21. *Ibid.*, p. 98.

22. Glasgow, *A Certain Measure*, p. 31.

23. *Ibid.*, p. 85.

24. Interview with Ellen Glasgow.

25. Glasgow, *A Certain Measure*, p. 61.

26. *Letters of Ellen Glasgow*, p. 70 (January 7, 1924).

27. Glasgow, *A Certain Measure*, p. 28.

28. *Ibid.* p. 27.

29. *Ibid.*, pp. 13-14.

30. *Ibid.*, pp. 16-17.

31. *Ibid.*, p. 17.

32. *Ibid.*, p. 94.

33. *Ibid.*, pp. vii-viii.

34. *Letters of Ellen Glasgow*, p. 240 (To Bessie Zaban Jones; May 9, 1938.).

35. Glasgow, *A Certain Measure*, pp. 146-47.

36. *Ibid.*, p. 146.

37. *Ibid.*, p. 149.

38. *Letters of Ellen Glasgow*, p. 30 (To Walter Hines Page; April 18, 1900.).

39. Glasgow, *A Certain Measure*, pp. 152-53.

40. *Ibid.*, p. 30.

41. Interview with Ellen Glasgow.

42. Glasgow, *A Certain Measure*, pp. 156-57.
43. *Ibid.*, pp. 160-61.
44. *Ibid.*, p. 12.
45. *Ibid.*, pp. 194, 197-98.
46. *Ibid.*, pp. 258-59.
47. *Letters of Ellen Glasgow*, p. 69 (August 23, 1923).
48. Interview with Ellen Glasgow.
49. Glasgow, *A Certain Measure*, p. 39.
50. *Letters of Ellen Glasgow*, p. 304 (To Bessie Zaban Jones; July 20, 1942.).
51. Glasgow, *A Certain Measure*, p. 34.
52. Interview with Ellen Glasgow.
53. Glasgow, *A Certain Measure*, p. 200.
54. [1] *Ibid.*
55. *Ibid.*, p. 41.
56. *Ibid.*
57. *Ibid.*, pp. 175-76.
58. Glasgow, *The Woman Within*, p. 123.
59. Interview with Ellen Glasgow.
60. Glasgow, *The Woman Within*, p. 124.
61. *Ibid.*, pp. 124-25.
62. *Ibid.*, p. 125.
63. *Ibid.*, pp. 126-27.
64. Glasgow, *A Certain Measure*, pp. 158-59.
65. Interview with Ellen Glasgow.
66. Glasgow, *A Certain Measure*, pp. 222-23.
67. *Ibid.*, p. 236.
68. *Ibid.*, p. 204.
69. *Letters of Ellen Glasgow*, p. 191 (Probably summer 1935).
70. Glasgow, *A Certain Measure*, p. 183.
71. *Ibid.*, pp. 183-84.
72. *Ibid.*, p. 262.
73. *Ibid.*
74. *Ibid.*, p. 205.
75. *Ibid.*, p. 206.
76. *Ibid.*, pp. 191-92.
77. *Letters of Ellen Glasgow*, pp. 116-17 (Probably spring, 1932.).

Chapter Three

1. Ellen Glasgow, *The Descendant* (New York, 1897), p. 19.
2. *Ibid.*, p. 107.
3. See the opening scenes in *The Voice of the People, The Deliverance,* and *Barren Ground*.

4. Glasgow, *The Descendant,* p. 3.
5. *Ibid.,* p. 71.
6. *Ibid.,* p. 63.

Chapter Four

1. "How common soldiers felt, I have never known, . . ."
Glasgow, *The Woman Within,* p. 233.
2. Glasgow, *A Certain Measure,* p. 31.
3. *Ibid.,* p. 34.
4. *Ibid.,* pp. 38-39.
5. *Ibid.,* p. 45.

Chapter Five

1. Glasgow, *A Certain Measure,* p. 70.
2. *Ibid.,* p. 69.

Chapter Six

1. Ellen Glasgow, *Virginia* (New York, 1913), p. 22.
2. *Letters of Ellen Glasgow,* p. 134.
3. Henry James and William Dean Howells also avoided too
intimate an investigation into the labyrinth of American business.
See James's *The American* and Howells's *The Rise of Silas Lapham.*
4. See *The Voice of the People* and *The Romance of a Plain Man.*

Chapter Seven

1. Glasgow, *A Certain Measure,* pp. 152-64.
2. *Ibid.,* pp. 129-30.

Chapter Eight

1. Ellen Glasgow, *The Romantic Comedians* (Garden City, N.Y.,
1926), p. 310.
2. *Ibid.,* p. 227.
3. *Ibid.,* p. 269.
4. Cf. Robert Holland, "Miss Glasgow's Prufrock," *American
Quarterly,* IX (Winter, 1957), 435-40.
5. Ellen Glasgow, *The Sheltered Life* (Garden City, N.Y., 1932),
p. 395.
6. *Ibid.,* p. 133. (Almost any Virginian can testify to the truth
of this description of ecclesiastical translation from "plain folk" to
"quality.")
7. *Ibid.,* pp. 385-86.

Chapter Nine

1. Glasgow, *A Certain Measure*, p. 249.
2. *Ibid.*, p. 250.
3. Ellen Glasgow, *In This Our Life* (New York, 1941), p. 466.
4. *Ibid.*, p. 394.
5. Glasgow, *A Certain Measure*, p. 249.
6. *Ibid.*, p. 253.
7. *Ibid.*, p. 264.

Chapter Ten

1. William W. Kelly, "Struggle for Recognition: a Study of the Literary Reputation of Ellen Glasgow." (Unpublished doctoral dissertation. Duke University, 1959), p. 18.
2. *The Critic*, XXVII (New Series) or XXX (Old Series), (May 22, 1897), 352, 353.
3. Kelly, *op. cit.*, p. 19.
4. *The Atlantic Monthly*, LXXXVI (Sept., 1900) 416-18.
5. *The Bookman*, XI (June, 1900), 397.
6. *The Outlook*, LXXI (May, 1902), 212.
7. *World's Work*, V (November, 1902), 2791.
8. Kelly, *op. cit.*, pp. 51-54.
9. *Ibid.*, p. 64.
10. *Ibid.*, p. 70.
11. Chalmers Roberts, "American Books in England," *World's Work*, VIII (October, 1904), 5430. (See Kelly, *op. cit.*, p. 71.).
12. Kelly, *op. cit.*, pp. 72-74.
13. *Ibid.*, pp. 85-86.
14. *The New York Times Book Review*, XIV (June 26, 1909), 402.
15. *The North American Review*, CXCIV (August, 1911), 302.
16. *The New York Times*, XVI (July 2, 1911), 414.
17. *Kelly, op. cit.*, pp. 141-43.
18. *Ibid.*, p. 157.
19. *The New York Times Book Review*, XXI (January 16, 1916), 17.
20. *The Nation*, CII (February 17, 1916), 197.
21. *The Literary Review* (November 17, 1923), 256.
22. Joyce Kilmer, *Literature in the Making* (New York, 1917), p. 229.
23. Carl Van Doren, *Contemporary American Novelists, 1900-1920* (New York, 1922), pp. 132-34.
24. Louise Maunsell Field, *Ellen Glasgow* (New York, 1923), p. 10.

Notes and References

25. Joseph Collins, *Taking the Literary Pulse* (New York, 1924), pp. 68-72.

26. Kelly, *op. cit.*, p. 216.

27. *The New York Herald Tribune Books* (April 19, 1925), 1.

28. *Ibid.*

29. *The Atlantic Monthly*, CXXXVI (August, 1925), 10.

30. *The Virginia Quarterly Review*, I (July, 1925), 261-64.

31. *The New York Herald Tribune Books*, II (September 12, 1926), 1.

32. *The American Mercury*, XVIII (October, 1929), 251.

33. Kelly, *op. cit.*, pp. 262-63.

34. *The Saturday Review of Literature*, XXIII (March 29, 1941), 1-2, 5.

35. *Time*, XXXVII (March 31, 1941), 72.

36. *The Virginia Quarterly Review*, XVII (Spring, 1941), 317-20.

37. "The Social Philosophy of Ellen Glasgow," *Social Forces*, IV (March, 1926), 495-503.

38. *The Women Who Make Our Novels* (New York, 1928), pp. 157-66.

39. *The Virginia Quarterly Review*, IX (1933), 595ff.

40. *The Saturday Review of Literature*, XVIII (September 10, 1938), 3.

41. *The New York Times Book Review* (December 18, 1938), 1.

42. *The Virginia Quarterly Review*, XVII (Summer, 1941), 405-17.

43. *College English*, III (October, 1941), 5.

44. Hamilton Basso, "Ellen Glasgow's Literary Credo," *The New York Times Book Review* (October 17, 1943), 5, 37.

45. *The New York Times Book Review* (October 30, 1955), 2.

Selected Bibliography

PRIMARY SOURCES

1. NOVELS

The Descendant. New York: Harper & Brothers, 1897.
Phases of an Inferior Planet. New York: Harper & Brothers, 1898.
The Voice of the People. New York: Doubleday, Page & Co., 1900.
The Battle-Ground. New York: Doubleday, Page & Co., 1902.
The Deliverance. New York: Doubleday, Page & Co., 1904.
The Wheel of Life. New York: Doubleday, Page & Co., 1906.
The Ancient Law. New York: Doubleday, Page & Co., 1908.
The Romance of a Plain Man. New York: The Macmillan Co. (later by Doubleday, Page & Co.),1909.
The Miller of Old Church. Garden City, N.Y.: Doubleday, Page & Co., 1911.
Virginia. Garden City, N.Y.: Doubleday, Page & Co., 1913.
Life and Gabriella. Garden City, N.Y.: Doubleday, Page & Co., 1916.
The Builders. Garden City, N.Y.: Doubleday, Page & Co., 1919.
One Man in His Time. Garden City, N.Y.: Doubleday, Page & Co., 1922.
Barren Ground. Garden City, N.Y.: Doubleday, Page & Co., 1925.
The Romantic Comedians. Garden City, N.Y.: Doubleday, Page & Co., 1926.
They Stooped to Folly. Garden City, N.Y.: Doubleday, Doran & Co., 1929.
The Sheltered Life. Garden City, N.Y.: Doubleday, Doran & Co., 1932.
Vein of Iron. New York: Harcourt, Brace & Co., 1935.
In This Our Life. New York: Harcourt, Brace & Co., 1941.
The Old Dominion Edition of the Works of Ellen Glasgow (Eight novels). Garden City, N.Y.: Doubleday, Doran & Co., 1929-1933.
The Virginia Edition of the Works of Ellen Glasgow (Twelve novels). New York: Charles Scribner's Sons, 1938.

2. SHORT STORIES

The Shadowy Third and Other Stories. Garden City, N.Y.: Doubleday, Page & Co., 1923.

3. OTHER VOLUMES

The Freeman and Other Poems. New York: Doubleday, Page & Co., 1902.

[148]

A Certain Measure: an Interpretation of Prose Fiction. New York: Harcourt, Brace & Co., 1943.
The Woman Within. New York: Harcourt, Brace & Co., 1954.
Letters of Ellen Glasgow, ed. Blair Rouse. New York: Harcourt, Brace & Co., 1958.

4. OTHER WRITINGS

"The Dynamic Past," *The Reviewer,"* I (March, 1921), 73-80.
"The Novel in the South," *Harper's Magazine,* CLXIII (December, 1928), 93-100.
"One Way to Write Novels," *Saturday Review of Literature,* XI (December 8, 1934), 334, 344, 350.
"What I Believe," *The Nation,* CXXXVI (April 12, 1933) 404-6.
"Heroes and Monsters," *Saturday Review of Literature,* XII (May 4, 1935), 3-4. The text of a speech delivered before the Friends of the Princeton Library, April 25, 1935.
"Elder and Younger Brother," *Saturday Review of Literature,* XV (January 23, 1937), 3-5. A variant form of a paper read for Ellen Glasgow by Allen Tate at a session of the Modern Language Association in Richmond in December, 1936.
"The Inscription," *Of Ellen Glasgow: an Inscribed Portrait.* New York: The Maverick Press, 1938.
"Ellen Glasgow," *I Believe: The Personal Philosophies of Certain Eminent Men and Women of Our Time,* ed. Clifton Fadiman. New York: Simon & Schuster, 1939 (pp. 93-110).

SECONDARY SOURCES

The articles and books listed below constitute a selection of materials which should be interesting and useful to the reader of Ellen Glasgow's fiction. For a much more extensive enumeration of pertinent Glasgow materials, the reader may consult the bibliographies in Frederick P. W. McDowell's *Ellen Glasgow and the Ironic Art of Fiction,* the relatively brief lists in Ellen Glasgow's *A Certain Measure,* the bibliographies by Egly and Quesenbery indicated below, and William W. Kelly's *An Ellen Glasgow Bibliography.*

ADAMS, J. DONALD. "The Novels of Ellen Glasgow," *New York Times Book Review,* December 18, 1939, pp. 1, 14. This review essay of *The Virginia Edition of the Works of Ellen Glasgow* and the other articles by Mr. Adams are thoughtful, informative accounts of the novelist and her work by a critic who was also her friend.
————. *The Shape of Books to Come.* New York: The Viking Press, 1944. Perceptive observations on Ellen Glasgow and her work.

BASSO, HAMILTON. "Ellen Glasgow's Literary Credo," *New York Times Book Review,* October 17, 1943, pp. 5, 37. A review of *A Certain Measure.* This essay pleased the novelist because she felt that Mr. Basso had understood what she meant in her fiction and in her book of criticism.

BENÉT, STEPHEN VINCENT and ROSEMARY. "Miss Ellen: A Rebel Against Regimentation," *New York Herald Tribune Books,* XVII (November 17, 1940), 7. A very useful article by two writers who understood Ellen Glasgow and appreciated her achievement.

BROOKS, VAN WYCK. *The Confident Years: 1885-1915.* New York: E. P. Dutton & Co., 1952. In a number of passages in this volume, but especially on pages 342-52, Mr. Brooks provides an appreciative, useful, and well-balanced assessment of Ellen Glasgow's contribution to American letters.

CABELL, JAMES BRANCH. "The Last Cry of Romance," *The Nation,* CXX (May 6, 1925), 521-22. One of the more thoughtful reviews of *Barren Ground* when it first appeared.

————. "Two Sides of the Shielded: a Note as to Ellen Glasgow," *Some of Us.* New York: Robert M. McBride & Co., 1930. Reminiscence of the long friendship of Cabell and Ellen Glasgow; it should be compared with some of Mr. Cabell's later observations.

————. "The Portrait," *Of Ellen Glasgow: An Inscribed Portrait.* New York: The Maverick Press, 1938. This typically Cabellian sketch of Ellen Glasgow appeared in a very limited edition. It is interesting, if perhaps more Cabell than Glasgow.

————. "Miss Glasgow of Virginia," *Let Me Lie.* New York: Farrar, Strauss & Co., 1947. Mr. Cabell's recollections; in general, they are friendly, if tart.

————. "Speaks with Candor of a Great Lady," *As I Remember It.* New York: The McBride Co., 1955. Mr. Cabell gets his revenge for Ellen Glasgow's unnecessary and unkind references to him in her autobiography, *The Woman Within.* His bitter treatment of his old friend is, however, neither fair nor justified.

CLARK, EMILY. "Appreciation of Ellen Glasgow and Her Work," *Virginia Quarterly Review,* V (April, 1929), 182-91. This article, somewhat revised, was later published in Miss Clark's *Innocence Abroad* (New York, 1931). It shows Ellen Glasgow as observed by a woman active in the literary world of America in the 1920's.

COLVERT, JAMES B. "Agent and Author: Ellen Glasgow's Letters to Paul Revere Reynolds," *Studies in Bibliography,* ed. Fredson Bowers, XIV, Papers of the Bibliographical Society of the University of Virginia. Charlottesville, Virginia, 1961; pp. 177-

96. These forty-one letters to Ellen Glasgow's literary agent are now in the Barrett Collection of the Alderman Library at the University of Virginia. These letters, unavailable when I prepared my edition of Ellen Glasgow's letters, are a welcome aid to further understanding of the novelist's career.

DAVIDSON, DONALD. "Another Woman Within," *New York Times Book Review,* January 19, 1958, pp. 7, 14. Review of *Letters of Ellen Glasgow;* shows this agrarian critic's interest in and understanding of the novelist.

EGLY, WILLIAM. "Bibliography of Ellen Anderson Gholson Glasgow," *Bulletin of Bibliography,* XVII (September-December, 1940), 47-50. A useful list, but one to be used with discretion.

EWING, MAJL. "The Civilized Uses of Irony: Ellen Glasgow." *English Studies in Honor of James Southall Wilson,* ed. Fredson Bowers. Charlottesville, Va.: University of Virginia Studies, IV, 1951; pp. 81-91. An excellent study of Ellen Glasgow's art and of the artist, with the emphases suggested by the title.

FADIMAN, CLIFTON. "Ellen Glasgow's South," *The New Republic,* LXXII (August 31, 1932), 79. Review of *The Sheltered Life* which deeply offended Ellen Glasgow; her ruffled feelings were soothed by the appearance the following week of a laudatory essay on her novel by her friend, Stark Young (q.v.).

FREEMAN, DOUGLAS SOUTHALL. "Ellen Glasgow: Idealist," *Saturday Review of Literature,* XII (August 31, 1935), 11-12. A very perceptive article by the late Virginia editor and historian who knew Ellen Glasgow well.

GARLAND, HAMLIN. " 'The Descendant' and Its Author," *Book Buyer,* XI (August, 1897), 45-46. Hamlin Garland was one of the first to congratulate the young author of *The Descendant;* this article is important as an early impression of Ellen Glasgow by a well-known writer.

GEISMAR, MAXWELL. "The Armor of the Legend," *Rebels and Ancestors: The American Novel, 1890-1915.* Boston: Houghton Mifflin Co., 1953. A Northern critic offers a somewhat severe but not unfair assessment.

HOFFMAN, FREDERICK J. *The Modern Novel in America, 1900-1950.* Chicago: Henry Regnery Co., 1951. Mr. Hoffman, one of our best scholar-critics, offers a fair, well-balanced account of Ellen Glasgow's contribution to the American novel.

HOLMAN, C. HUGH. "Ellen Glasgow and the Southern Literary Tradition," *Virginia in History and Tradition:* Institute of Southern Culture Lectures at Longwood College, 1957, ed. R. C. Simonini, Jr. Farmville, Virginia, 1958. An informative essay defining the nature and meaning of the literary tradition in the

South and asserting Ellen Glasgow's right to be considered within, not outside, that tradition.

HUBBELL, JAY B. "Ellen Glasgow," *The South in American Literature: 1607-1900.* Durham, N.C.: Duke University Press, 1954. One of the most eminent of American literary historians assesses Ellen Glasgow's achievement in relation to the whole development of literature in the South.

JONES, HOWARD MUMFORD. "Battalions of Women," *Virginia Quarterly Review,* VIII (October, 1932), 591-94. This review of *The Sheltered Life* expresses the opinions of a scholar-critic who was a friend of Ellen Glasgow and whose judgment she valued.

————. "Ellen Glasgow, Witty, Wise, and Civilized," *New York Herald Tribune Books,* XIV (July 24, 1938), 1-2. Friendly, informative, and perceptive review of *The Virginia Edition of the Novels of Ellen Glasgow.*

————. "Product of the Tragic Muse." *Saturday Review of Literature,* XXIII (March 29, 1941), 5. An excellent estimate of *In This Our Life.*

————. "The Regional Eminence of Ellen Glasgow," *Saturday Review of Literature,* XXVI (October 16, 1943), 20. A stimulating comment on *A Certain Measure* and on Ellen Glasgow's achievement as a novelist.

KAZIN, ALFRED. *On Native Grounds.* New York: Reynal & Hitchcock, 1942. Mr. Kazin's treatment of Ellen Glasgow in his critical study of American prose writing is well balanced and generally favorable.

KELLY, WILLIAM W. *An Ellen Glasgow Bibliography.* Charlottesville: The University of Virginia Press, 1963. This excellent enumerative and descriptive bibliography supersedes other bibliographies of Ellen Glasgow and provides a much-needed aid to the study of the novelist.

KILMER, JOYCE. "'Evasive Idealism' Handicaps Our Literature," *New York Times Magazine,* March 5, 1916, p. 10. Reprinted as "Evasive Idealism in Literature" in *Literature in the Making,* ed. Joyce Kilmer. New York: Harper & Brothers, 1917. The poet of "Trees" interviews the lover of dogs and hater of the variety of sentimentality she labeled "evasive idealism." An interesting article for these associations.

MARCOSSON, ISAAC F. *Before I Forget: A Pilgrimage to the Past.* New York: Dodd, Mead & Co., 1959. This experienced newspaperman's memories provide interesting comment on his impressions of the novelist.

MCDOWELL, FREDERICK P. W. "Ellen Glasgow and the Art of the

Novel," *Philological Quarterly*, XXX (July, 1951), 328-47. A valuable essay by one of the more perceptive of Glasgow critics.
————. *Ellen Glasgow and the Ironic Art of Fiction*. Madison, Wisconsin: University of Wisconsin Press, 1960. This excellent, full-length critical study of Ellen Glasgow's theory and practice of the art of the novel should be read by everyone interested in Ellen Glasgow and in fiction.

MENCKEN, H. L. "A Southern Skeptic," *The American Mercury*, XXIX (August, 1933), 504-6. An interesting review by the sage of Baltimore of Ellen Glasgow's *Old Dominion Edition* of her novels.

MIMS, EDWIN. "The Social Philosophy of Ellen Glasgow," *Social Forces*, IV (March, 1926), 494-503. Reprinted in Dr. Mims's *The Advancing South*. Garden City, N.Y., 1926. An assessment of Ellen Glasgow as social historian in fiction and of her social thought by a Southern scholar who admired the author and her work.

MONROE, N. ELIZABETH. "Contemplations of Manners in Ellen Glasgow," *The Novel and Society*. Chapel Hill, N.C.: University of North Carolina Press, 1941. Ellen Glasgow did *not* like this consideration of herself and her work; she thought it imperceptive.

PATTERSON, DANIEL W. "Ellen Glasgow's Plan for a Social History of Virginia." *Modern Fiction Studies*, V (Winter, 1959-1960), 353-60. This essay inquires into the problem as to whether Ellen Glasgow deliberately "planned" her social history of Virginia in the form of fiction early in her career or imposed the concept of such a plan upon the novels much later (as Cabell believed).

PERKINS, MAXWELL E. *Editor to Author: the Letters of Maxwell Perkins*, ed. John Hall Wheelock. New York: Charles Scribner's Sons, 1950. Maxwell Perkins was associated wth Ellen Glasgow in preparing the Virginia Edition of her novels.

QUESENBERY, W. D., JR. "Ellen Glasgow: a Critical Bibliography," *Bulletin of Bibliography and Magazine Notes*, XXII (May-August, September-December, 1959), 201-6, 230-36. A revision and an extension of the bibliography by William H. Egly published in *Bulletin of Bibliography*, XVII (September, 1940), 47-50 (q.v.). A useful list to be used with discretion.

QUINN, ARTHUR HOBSON. "Ellen Glasgow and the New South," *American Fiction: an Historical and Critical Survey*. New York: D. Appleton-Century Co., 1936. Interesting for views of Ellen Glasgow by one of the more distinguished historians of American fiction.

RAWLINGS, MARJORIE KINNAN. "Regional Literature of the South," *College English*, I (February, 1940), 381-89. The novelist friend of Ellen Glasgow comments on the regional aspects of Southern writing, including that by Miss Glasgow.

ROUSE, BLAIR. "Time and Place in Southern Fiction," *The Hopkins Review*, VI (Fall, 1952), 37-61. Reprinted in *Southern Renascence: the Literature of the Modern South*, eds. Louis D. Rubin, Jr., and Robert D. Jacobs. Baltimore: The Hopkins Press, 1953. Contains material on Ellen Glasgow's treatment of time and place.

————. Introduction, *Letters of Ellen Glasgow*. New York: Harcourt, Brace & Co., 1958. Sketches Ellen Glasgow's achievement in relation to her letters and other autobiographical writings.

RUBIN, LOUIS D., JR. *No Place on Earth: Ellen Glasgow, James Branch Cabell and Richmond-in-Virginia*. Austin, Texas: University of Texas Press, 1959. Excessively disparaging of Ellen Glasgow if occasionally perceptive.

SHERMAN, STUART PRATT. "Ellen Glasgow: The Fighting Edge of Romance," New York *Herald Tribune Books*, I (April 19, 1925), 1-3. Reprinted in *Critical Woodcuts*. New York: Charles Scribner's Sons, 1926. One of the most significant comments on *Barren Ground* and one which pleased the novelist very much.

STEELE, OLIVER L. "Ellen Glasgow, Social History, and the 'Virginia Edition,'" *Modern Fiction Studies*, VII (Summer, 1961), 173-76. Refutes Daniel W. Patterson's notions concerning Ellen Glasgow's ideas for social history in fiction as set forth in his earlier article (q.v.). Mr. Steele's observations are valuable as offering more than simple refutations; they suggest how the idea of social history functioned in Ellen Glasgow's work.

WILSON, JAMES SOUTHALL. "Ellen Glasgow's Novels," *Virginia Quarterly Review*, IX (October, 1933), 595-600. This review essay on the *Old Dominion Edition* and the other essays by Dr. Wilson, listed below, reveal the scholar and sometime editor of the *Virginia Quarterly Review* offering assessments of Ellen Glasgow and her work. Dr. Wilson was the novelist's admiring friend as well as clear-seeing critic over many years.

————. "Two American Novels," *Virginia Quarterly Review*, XL (October, 1935), 620-26. Review of *Vein of Iron*.

————. "Ellen Glasgow: Ironic Idealist," *Virginia Quarterly Review*, XV (Winter, 1939), 121-26. Essay-review of the *Virginia Edition*.

————. "Ellen Glasgow: 1941," *Virginia Quarterly Review*, XVII (Winter, 1941) 317-20. Review of *In This Our Life*.

————. "Ellen Glasgow's Autobiography," *Virginia Quarterly Review*, XXXI (Spring, 1955), 292-98. Review of *The Woman Within*.

————. "Ellen Glasgow's Letters," *Virginia Quarterly Review*,

XXXIV (Summer, 1958), 455-59. Review of *Letters of Ellen Glasgow*.

WOODWARD, C. VANN. "Bonds of Mind and Spirit." *A History of the South: Origins of the New South, 1877-1913*. Ed Wendell Holmes Stephenson and E. Merton Coulter. IX. Baton Rouge: Louisiana State University Press, 1951. A distinguished historian shows the importance of Ellen Glasgow's earlier novels for an understanding of "the New South."

YOUNG, STARK. "Deep South Notes VI: At Sheltered Valley." *The New Republic*, LXXII (September 7, 1932), 100-2. Stark Young, novelist, critic, and friend of Ellen Glasgow, discussed *The Sheltered Life* in this essay; his remarks helped to soothe the novelist's feelings so deeply stirred by Clifton Fadiman's review in the same journal (q.v.).

Index

47224

Proust, Marcel, 28
Pulitzer Prize, 13, 135, 136

Queen Victoria, 117

Rawlings, Majorie, Kinnan, 26, 27, 142
Rebecca, 85
Rebels and Ancestors, 137
Review of Reviews, 134
Rice, Alice Hegan, 132
Richardson, Samuel, 28
Rise of Silas Lapham, The, 145
Roberts, Chalmers, 146
Roberts, Elizabeth Madox, 26, 94

Sandburg, Carl, 27
Saturday Review of Literature, The, 13, 26, 143, 147
Schelling, F. W. J. von, 29
Schopenhauer, Arthur, 29
Scott, Sir Walter, 28, 46, 53
Sherman, Stuart Pratt, 134
Smith, Adam, 29
Smollett, Tobias, 28
So Big, 134
Social Forces, 147
"Social Philosophy of Ellen Glasgow, The," 147
So Red the Rose, 55
Sound and the Fury, The, 141
South in American Literature, The, 137
Southern Renascence, 137
Spencer, Herbert, 29
Spinoza, Benedict, 29
Sterne, Laurence, 28
Stevenson, Robert Louis, 28
"Struggle for Recognition: a Study of the Literary Reputation of Ellen Glasgow," 146
Surry of Eagle's Nest, 55
Swinnerton, Frank, 12, 26

Tate, Allen, 26, 32, 81
Tess of the D'Urbervilles, 70
Thoreau, Henry David, 115
Three Sisters, The, 44
Time magazine, 135, 147
Time of Man, The, 26, 94
Toksvig, Signe, 26
Tolstoy, Leo, 28
Towne, Charles Hanson, 26
"Trees," 133
Trojan Women, The, 135
Turgenev, Ivan, 28
Tutwiler, Col. C. C., Jr., 142

Under the Greenwood Tree, 70
Une Vie, 41
Unvanquished, The, 140

Van Doren, Carl, 133, 146
Van Doren, Mrs. Irita, 26
Van Vechten, Carl, 26, 134
Virginia Quarterly Review, The, 25, 134, 147
Virginian, The, 132

Wagenknecht, Edward, 137
Walpole, Hugh, 12, 27, 38
Waverley novels, 28
Well of Loneliness, The, 27
Wharton, Edith, 18, 26, 63, 97, 134
Whicher, George F., 137
Wilde, Oscar, 47
Wilson, James Southall, 25, 31, 135, 136
Wister, Owen, 132
Women Who Make Our Novels, The, 147
Woolf, Virginia, 27, 28
World's Work, The, 131, 146

Young, Stark, 26, 31, 42, 55

Zola, Emile, 46

DATE DUE

GAYLORD

PRINTED IN U.S.A.